THE
POSSIBLE
MAN

THE POSSIBLE MAN

LIFE IN THE SHADOW OF THE JUST

MEIR MICHEL ABEHSERA

SWAN
HOUSE
PUBLISHING

For permission requests, email to the publisher,
Info@SwanHousePublishing.com

For additional information on the author visit:
MEIRABEHSERA.COM

ISBN# 978-0692047453

Printed in the USA

Book Design by Haki Abehsera
Photo by Sarah Abehsera Zohar

INTRODUCTION

SIMCHA GOTTLIEB

In the early 1970s I was co-owner of a restaurant, a funky little macrobiotic hangout in upstate New York called Belly of the Whale. One wintry Saturday afternoon I took off from work to run a few errands, leaving the business in the capable hands of my partner. Along the way I stopped to pick something up at the home of our friends Michel and Claude.

Michel had become my mentor in natural medicine, its culinary arts, and its spiritual underpinnings. He was not yet regularly using his Hebrew name Meir, but was already well into a process of reclaiming his childhood devotion to the Judaism of his illustrious forebears, a long line of Moroccan holy men. But what I loved most about the Abehseras was the robust warmth of their unfragmented family.

They were all sitting around the big oak table in the dining room—father and mother, their two young daughters, and several guests (there were *always* guests). Michel welcomed me and bade me come sit next to him. Reaching across the table to a large serving platter, he spooned a measure of its still-warm contents into a dish and said, here, Steve, you must taste this.

I'd never seen anything quite like it; a stew of sorts, whose ingredients were at first glance indecipherable except for the obvious presence of some chickpeas. A mound of what looked like a pudding proved on further investigation to be soft brown rice that had been wrapped in cheesecloth and slow-cooked in the same pot as the stew. Its texture and taste were of the earth, but not of this world; aromatic and darkly bold, yet comforting as baby food and nuanced with grace notes of stratospheric lightness. Wow. I looked up and Michel was watching me with knowing eyes. I looked over across the table toward Claude, who had no doubt whipped up this better-than-ambrosia masterwork. She deflected my gaze with a quiet inner smile and resumed laughing with her kids.

Dafina, they call it. Though ingredients vary—grain, meat, chickpeas, prunes, and cumin are commonly included—the key to this concoction is not so much in the selection of substances but in the timing. Prepared on Friday afternoon, the mélange is slow-cooked overnight and served at the Saturday meal, as the family gathers to bask in the timeless sanctity of *Shabbat*.

It would be a cheap shot to say that that plate of *dafina* changed my life; it did not. But I did sense something magical at that intersection of tradition and the table—something that would yet take me a couple of years to digest. I eventually discovered how that simple dish had been my first taste of what Meir Michel Abehsera calls the *possible*.

Meir's lectures, sometimes in our restaurant and sometimes in a home, were always freewheeling and unpredictable. We first had encountered him as the author of *Zen Macrobiotic Cooking*, and got to know him while he was writing *Cooking for Life* (later revised and reissued as *Cooking with Care and Purpose*). Ostensibly he was our foodie guru, a teacher of natural healing through eating in harmony with the environment. As it turned out, that environment proved to be way bigger than a mere ecosystem or planet. Wending his own way, he shared his gains and losses and guided us along a path from the biological to the spiritual, not by quantum leaps but by human-sized steps, tapping the ground as we went. Occasionally he'd stand there in silence as if deciding what to speak about, then turn to one of us and say, you're giving the lecture tonight. Trial by fire, keeping it real.

Years passed, and as Meir's thought and talks evolved, his sphere of influence grew exponentially. In 1980 he called me—we were living in different cities by then—and told me about a new project. A friend, a fan of his lectures, had been badgering him about transcribing and adapting his talks into a book. Now, anyone familiar with Meir's lyrical, inscrutable way of challenging, inspiring, enthralling and confounding a roomful of truth seekers could testify as to how ridiculous an idea that must have seemed at the time. But the transcripts were recorded nonetheless. He had begun to sort through them to find some semblance of linear structure upon which to expand, and found himself adrift in a turbulent sea. Would I come and help him edit the book? Ever the glutton for punishment, I told him I'd be there as soon as my current commitment was done.

In the fourth chapter of *The Possible Man,* Meir describes the method of an editor:

> *He cannot settle for fragments of truth taken out of context. He puts pieces together, sifting through everything he finds, until, after years of tests and trials, he comes up with a sum of the parts, a wholesomeness that leads him directly to the Divine. He will not kneel until the revelation is complete.*

Some might consider that an impossibly high standard. But to Meir it was fundamental; just another prerequisite exercise in the pursuit of the possible. So for the next several years, I worked with him on the book, part-time or full-time depending on our fortunes, fortitude, and family demands. The lectures, as he had suspected from the get-go, were too phantasmagorical to find a comfortable place on the page. But they provided seeds, and we weeded and watered. I watched him reach deep into fathomless recesses of inchoate memory and struggle to emerge with words that would make sense. During my tenure there was no completion and no kneeling. Other editors came and went after my time. The work soared higher and plunged lower. When the book was finally finished and published in 1992, there were passages that were refreshingly unfamiliar to me. It read to me as a conversation with an old friend who had grown immeasurably, yet in essence hadn't changed. Rereading it today, every sentence is new, and rings true.

Not that it's an easy read. For Meir, the *possible* does not preclude a compelling, at times overwhelming awareness of an impossibly sublime dimension of reality. When he speaks about playing by the rules and living within limits—as, for example, in his account of the lesson he learned as a young boy playing with marbles—the reader is treated to a glimpse of an entirely unbounded vision, an almost superhuman set of skills. He is forever pushing the envelope beyond pedestrian norms, yet the net effect is to guide us in the fine art of putting one foot in front of the other. He shares an early childhood experience of oscillating in and out of existence, triggered by an otherwise mundane change. He describes a feverish vision in his late teens of other-worldly angelic visitors—a vision that defined his life's purpose. He segues from his very real, well-documented reputation as the "Rebbe's Whistler" to an extended fantasy of magical realism worthy of a Reb Nachman or a Borges (two of his favorite storytellers, holy and profane) wherein he is transformed from poet to critic to barking dog to buffoon and back again.

Meir used to say that the surest sign of genuine hospitality is when someone walking in off the street could look around the house and be unable to tell who are the guests and who is the host. *The Possible Man* is in many ways an extension, in book form, of the Abehsera home—a city of refuge, an oasis, a stimulating salon, and a comfort zone for the estranged and displaced. He invites us in and allows us to stake our claim.

So come play a while in the amusement park of Meir's metaphors. His bizarre cast of characters will soon become familiar friends. Some will no doubt reveal themselves to have been *ourselves*, all along. His parables are not quickly deciphered; nor should they be, for they are meant to be rewritten in our own lives. Their mystic significance may at times be almost obvious; but only obliquely does Meir spill the beans. He trusts us to gain the wisdom he is offering on our own.

Make yourself at home. Pull up a chair to this well-laid table. There's plenty of food, and the kitchen is open all night. And as with whole grains, so with these words: I expect Meir would recommend that we chew well before swallowing.

Heaven is the room next door
to the one who greets the stranger
hate is unknown to the man
whose heart is one large chamber

*Only a father as good as mine
could have taught me with silence
all that I have tried to accomplish
here with noise, in these pages,
which I dedicate to his memory.*

PART ONE

The Boatman

The Smuggler

The Well and the Spring

Breaking the Vessels

Making Room

Beyond the Frontier

The High Road

1

ON COMING to America with the intention to write a novel. * On relinquishing that dream to go on cooking for the ill. * On discovering how food is more eloquent than words. * Writing books on health and medicine. * Becoming an authority on the subject. * Leaving the scene after discovering a different type of medicine: the medicine for the soul. * Searching for the proper word to effect durable cures in this new field. * On being a boatman: transporting knowledge from one place to another, and making out of man a bridge.

THE BOATMAN

A FTER WE arrived in America in 1964, my wife and I became active in endeavors where the mind finds more solace in a bowl of wholesome food than from any given mode of thinking. I wrote books on nutrition and natural medicine. I gave impassioned speeches about the benefits of healthy eating. My wife put those teachings in their true perspective by preparing spectacular meals for the table.

The priority was to stand by the sick and concoct the best possible cure. I recall only a natural inclination to help alleviate pain, and we went quickly to work with very little awareness of doing so. We saw a raging fire and entered the chain to pass the bucket.

In those days my concern bordered on fanaticism. I was often tempted to stop strangers on the street and invite them home for a healthy meal. In fact, our house was always filled with people who sought physical or psychological support, who paid more attention to what we put on the table than to what we thought. Though I had come to America with the intention of starting a novel, I soon found that I had swapped the magic of the word for the healing power of food. Most of the guests would eat in silence. We knew better than to engage in empty discourse with those in crisis. Food spoke more eloquently than words.

No more literature then. I wrote cookbooks instead. But I gained much in the trade-off. The change seasoned my thinking. It touched off a small revolution in my understanding of the way the intellect operates. Specifically, it made me more acutely aware of a sense of priority through which intelligence gains pertinence. I had to be struck by the evidence that we grow in wisdom when we use only that which is most effective. But it is never easy. You have to silence every other voice, however intelligent and tempting it may be, and select a less grandiose means. As you remain in the background, busying yourself with the urgencies of the day, intelligence naturally grows within you. You are paid back many times for your services. It is as though the physical exertion has given rise to a corresponding measure of metaphysical growth. As far as you know, you are as poor as ever. You can never be sure that a reward is waiting somewhere for you. Yet, when you are faced with a situation some day that would normally demand prodigious intellectual exertion, you are able to resolve it with a slight turn of thought. You have become the person they call upon to crack safes.

It is evident that the priority should not automatically be on the side of action. Neither, for that matter, should it be exclusively on the side of thought. It is not even the most astute balance of the two. Rather, it is another unrelated and quite undefined force which breaks forth to do the work. Perhaps it is thought turned silent, sacrificing itself so as to emerge as a deed. Or a force could be born out of a stir of the soul; a sort of unplanned, unhesitating act which pours forth with the strength of unbridled will. It may well be an overabundance of joy that erupts from the depths of being. Whatever its character, this irresistible, nameless force will cause one who is timid to deliver an explosive speech. It will prompt the wicked to kick the habit. It will scream perfectly composed stanzas into the poet's ear. It will empower a small country such that it can scare a band of belligerent nations out of their shoes. At times it will appear with a certain air of madness that will compel the most wise to behave like buffoons.

It must have been that same force that motivated my wife and I to attend to the sick. For we were not all that experienced. In France, I had rid myself of various ailments through certain effective methods of cure. Suddenly, here in America, we were caught up in the teaching of those methods. At first it was in private consultations, then later in speaking to large gatherings. The lectures were transcribed and edited into books, all written and published in a relatively short time, in the manner of a short-order cook preparing fast dishes. What we lacked in maturity was made up for with enthusiasm.

It is ironic that with so little wisdom I could have been considered an authority on the subject. I was no polished expert by any standard. But I served my term with commitment and tried to speak between the lines to motivate the reader to search for a still better cure. The books and lectures were enough to begin a dialogue. I stuttered, but spoke with my soul.

Twenty-five years ago only a handful of us were familiar with natural medicine. Now there are literally thousands who know as much as I do. As a result, I have no feeling of guilt about leaving the scene. I consider myself free to shift my priority to what would please my heart most, which is to speak of a certain medicine for the soul. Here, however, there are no blood and veins, no clear system or vital signs to proclaim definitively how the medicine heals. One has to establish tangible criteria, or run the risk of being called an occultist. There are many masters of illusion working in this field. Without the proper terms in which to speak, one might be taken for a charlatan. Technicians of the occult might speak of "light" as though they owned it. Care must be taken when attempting to expose the dividing line between the real and the make-believe.

In this domain, I am required to wrestle with illusion. Victory here is deceptive. You cannot honestly say that you have won. Illusion, having no ground upon which to stand, never bites the dust. You can never tell who has the upper hand. On the field of battle, all is clouds. You can scarcely see the position of the enemy.

You think you have reached the top when, in fact, you have descended into the pit. The enemy will claim victory, no matter what happens. For my part, I can only claim a day's work. I am like one of the foot soldiers who has fought well enough to be paid for his fortitude, regardless of the outcome of the battle.

My speaking engagements on physical health were never quite what they had been advertised to be. Although I was expected to speak strictly on that subject, the discussions invariably strayed to less material concerns. The room would cry for a more metaphysical kind of mending. I scraped all the answers I could find from my poor reserves. What was really happening at those congenial gatherings? It was one of those inevitable episodes in everyone's youth where he unwittingly allows himself to be transported higher than gravity would have him stand. Then he runs out of fuel and hangs there, anguished, not even knowing that he is in midair. No wonder he feels alienated; he is not in his place. What he needs is to come down for repair and then take a safer journey. It is this maneuver which I have dubbed the "possible".

The idea of a book based on these lectures came up often, but I would dismiss it. The page is a very flat place. It can't reproduce the sounds of human interaction. The exchanges that take place in a room full of people impregnate the flesh with memory. The body vibrates to immeasurable decibels long after the gathering has ended. The eye is favored with sceneries which cancel inner torment. The colors wash the soot off of us from dark moments of solitude.

The writer who has not sunk beneath the waves formed by a live audience is not confronted with the challenge of having to transmute perspiration into words. He can cheat, and no one will care, because there are no witnesses present in whose heat truth is hatched. With an audience, the faces keep reminding the speaker to come back to his true self, to go neither beyond nor below his situation. There is constant feedback, eye contact, instantaneous adjustment. People see you dip below the wave and above it again. They cannot wait to see you come back. They are on your side. They want you to succeed. There is genuine growth on both sides. Humility and love are *de rigueur*. How can the page be so impudent as to presume to do the same?

Years went by, but the idea of a book kept surfacing. Meanwhile, the nature of the talks changed in parallel with my personal growth. I had begun to take a more active interest in my own tradition. My life became more defined as I immersed myself in the study of Jewish sacred books. Study and prayer took increasingly more time away from my practice of natural medicine. That "metaphysical mending" became of primary concern to me and was reflected in the themes of my public talks. But the need for a book dogged me. Around the same time, a friend proposed to me that a book could be made by simply transcribing my lectures. Still I did not budge, for I had no time for such an undertaking. But he persisted, insisting that with the transcription completed, all that would be needed was a simple editing job. Easily said. I tried to explain how the spoken word usually lands lifeless on the page, that it gathers dust quickly in print, that it would need extensive revision to give it presence. But my friend prevailed upon me, maintaining that it could all be done in six months. I finally believed him, and proceeded to turn my life upside down.

For years, I watched hordes of ideas being rejected by the yellow pad. Their vitality was only oral. Now I can only hope that those which made it onto these pages will be able to rise up to dissolve the darkness from before the reader's eyes. Heaven only knows if they will achieve their mission. It has been my ambition to transpose whatever sacred substance comes my way to places where it has never been, without diminishing its impact or marring the meaning it has at home. The sacred kept slipping away from my hand; that is its nature. It does not always acquiesce to dress in foreign garb.

In these texts, I have worked mostly as a boatman. I did not wait to become rich or wise before giving over what I received. I gave everything I possessed on the very day I received it. The idea, however, is not exactly mine. It is a sage's command. The way I understood it was that all I had to do was keep alive in myself the will to share, and he would take care of the rest. Although no specifics were enunciated, I understood it perfectly to be a promise that he, the sage, would be my storehouse. To this day, my role has been to transport "a priceless merchandise." What a wondrous bridge man is!

2

ON COMMUNICATING the eternal relevance of the sacred through anomalous ways. * Awakening the stolid mind with the *madness of the holy.* * On how our own faults make of us potential smugglers. * Faults as decoys; the customs guards are fooled. They think the Jew, the quintessential smuggler, is a throwback, when he has never been so alive. * On speaking to the child with the intent to smuggle wisdom to the man who towers above him. * Finally, a few words on how the deed tests the validity of thought, and how true adventure is in the known.

THE SMUGGLER

I AM A SMUGGLER. This has been my trade for years. It is a habit that I have developed in my attempt to understand and to communicate the eternal relevance of the sacred. The quality of communication has been so poor that all messages are either deflected or distorted. Spiritual language has become corrupt. The terminology has been usurped or degraded. It has become embarrassing to use the words which were once our own, but have been defiled in the mouths of shoddy characters. So we are forced to develop a new mode of expression, one that will leap over the heads of our detractors and defy imitation. It is a voice that cannot be duplicated because it speaks in the language of the soul. It is a language that Jewish mystics have called the "madness of the holy." Its main role is to awaken the stolid mind. It comes with speed to penetrate deep inside the listener until he flutters like a flame. Its wavelength is subtle. Anyone angry or hateful cannot possibly decode such dialogue. The detractors see my mouth forming words but they cannot hear. Even the simplest meaning eludes them. Yet there is nothing magical about this type of speech. In fact, it is just our peculiar

manner of speaking, and whoever finds it convoluted has simply lost his sense of wonder.

Smuggler. I call it that frankly only to disarm an accuser from tagging me wrongly with such an appellation. In this context, in the commerce of thoughts, smuggling is an honorable function. It may seem that I speak in an elusive manner, but I am not so complicated.

It is in response to the thickness of exile that I have to let my soul speak the language that pleases it, or else drown in conventions and niceties. In this exile, as in any other, when a Jew speaks, he smuggles wisdom. It is a special flight of the soul, an *entente* between souls, a madness we use in emergencies when the heart is too dead to listen to reason. To make use of the *madness of the holy*, one must step out of the limitations of the profane and begin to dance the holy dance, dipping one foot in light and one foot in darkness. As we leap over the dividing line, we smuggle the fallen sparks of exile beneath the soles of our feet.

The smuggler's art lies latent in every one of us, waiting to be activated. We all use it, if unconsciously, to a degree. Intelligence itself is a smuggler. One of its skills is to convey as much information as possible with a minimum number of words. Often it speaks like a poet who knows *not* to telegraph the meaning of his words. Intelligence knows the exact place of silence in the verse. It knows when to break the news in an ancient text. Sometimes, a verse speaks more eloquently when it ages. For is it not every good writer's desire to meet the reader anytime, anywhere?

The ordinary reader often makes the best smuggler. Smuggling is not necessarily a craft practiced by the sophisticated. I would explain to the ordinary person that there is this old locomotive which is parked in a big yard where all trains puff smoke and take on provisions. It is me. I am the locomotive, and I would show him how the boxcars behind me are loaded with wounds and scars and all the faults that I have learned to live with. To achieve at least some small measure of peace as I hear them moaning, I begin to move and let out a blast of my steam whistle to smother their din.

My faults outnumber me. I have become so small by comparison, that without all this freight I would surely look like a mite on the track. But I consider my faults a blessing, as they assist me in diverting the attention of those who wish to do me harm. Because, in truth, this train carries a priceless cargo. I have brought my faults along only to serve as a decoy, to help me make it past the frontier. Had I officially stripped myself of all my defects it would have been impossible for me to make the slightest move. My faults serve as a camouflage. By assuming the colors of the landscape, I am able to fool the customs guards. They search my baggage, but find nothing, for I have disguised my cargo as bags of stones. The guards, crisp and efficient, swagger and wink among themselves, concealing their scorn for this unkempt, unfashionable immigrant. "Let the Jew take his last trip," they say. But the irony is mine. They think they are sending me off to die; in fact, I have never been so alive. With an absurd and automatic "Much obliged," I move on.

I address myself to the adult, with the wish that at the same time I will strike a chord with the child who dwells within the adult. The child's nature is to want to be taken by the fable, though he knows you are keeping a moral or a lesson for the end. But to keep his attention you must be sure that the story's chain of events flows easily into the moral and that you do not suddenly spell out the lesson too soon, spoiling everything. The child is willing to make himself even more childlike in order to make room for the wonder. He won't allow his cleverness to interfere until the tale is completed. He knows the code of illusion. He knows it is the time for listening, not for questions.

There is often a moral that emerges in these collected pieces, for there is no tale told by a human that is not replete with morals. However, I have other intentions, very specific intentions to rouse the listener to practice the *mitzvah*, the deed, without which even the best of thought is a mere clamor of the mind. The deed is designed to test the validity of thought, to pursue and confront every thought and force it to prove itself. It is the special function of deeds to harness themselves to visions and dreams and thus render them possible.

In that sense, the journey I propose is very real. Its road is traveled on foot. The exceptions are those impulsive moments when the soul breaks its fetters and leaps into flight. And even in those moments of rapture, there is control. Eyes will not roll back in their sockets from an overflow of the spirit. The traveler is encouraged to test me, to tap the ground as we proceed.

It is a familiar road, one that I as a Jew have been traveling for thousands of years. Nonetheless, I am still dazed by the sights as if they were new; for the greatest adventure is into the known. It begins and ends with one companion, one book, one God. It is not constant changes of direction or contrived excursions into the unfathomable. For the Jew, adventure is actualization of what already is. Even on the beaten path, there is sufficient room in which to get lost. But familiar though it may be, it is still broad enough to accommodate the infinite.

3

WHERE ANCIENT sages foresee exile and gather together to deliberate on which kind of course their teachings are to follow; in the manner of the well or that of the spring. Their main concern is that they do not want their teachings to fall into the hands of the usurpers. Therefore, they opt for the austere well. * After 1,500 years, the Baal Shem Tov comes to change that decision, and introduces the ways of the spring. * Hasidut is born. It comes to complete the work of Kabbala, its ancient parent. Just like the Kabbala, it meets with resistance. Meanwhile, Hasidut proves to be a potent medicine for the soul. For it makes one wise and flattens vanity, and it does break heavy masks through laughter.

THE WELL AND THE SPRING

MONG THE MANY disciples of Rabbi Yochanan there were two who outweighed all the rest each in his own way. Rabbi Yochanan was wont to compare one of them, Rabbi Eliezer, to a *well*, and the other, Rabbi Elazar, to a *spring*. The well, apart from faithfully preserving that which is entrusted to its care, affords its contents time to acquire character. But the always renewed, ever-flowing waters of the spring travel far to refresh whomever they find along their path. These two modes of teaching and their impact on history serve as the main inspiration for this chapter.

It is traditional Jewish belief that the generation that lived in Moses' time had more insight into the sacred than we do. They were closer to the Source. They had witnessed God's miracles in Egypt and at Sinai. The extravagance of these miracles did not offend the intellect. The spirit hovered naturally over the physical. Faith was in the flesh. Matter had clear visions of the Divine.

Our disadvantage is certain; but we are somewhat privileged. We have been put in a situation where we are forced to try harder. We work blind. Heaven appreciates our efforts and seems to have reserved for itself the right to withhold vital details until they are revealed, each one in its appropriate time. It is a subtle smuggling, a heavenly engineered one this time. Each phase coincides perfectly with the needs of the time. One phase is pregnant with another. Still waters turn suddenly into springs to deliver the new message.

At times the change of pace happens naturally, with the seasons; and at other times the leaders of the generation gather to deliberate over which kind of course the teachings are to follow. One memorable instance was in Talmudic times, seventeen centuries ago, when an assembly of sages put to a vote the question of whether certain teachings, which form the Oral Law, should be preserved, gathered as water in a well, or allowed to pour out like a flowing spring. Their main concern was that the teachings should not fall into the hands of usurpers who would use them for wrong ends. They also foresaw the impending long exile, so they had to apply themselves to search for the safest mode of transportation over time. They opted for the well. Subsequently, the knowledge was handed over to those who were judged worthy of containing it, and that became the established order. It lasted some fifteen hundred years, during which time the waters were enriched through contact with the stone, thus acquiring an excellence they would not have absorbed above ground.

Then, during the eighteenth century in Poland, the holy Baal Shem Tov, founder of the *Hasidic* movement, came to establish a different course. It had become essential that the spring take over. Through him, the waters were to emerge from their cache to chase after redemption. The waters trickled at first. Then they became rivulets, then brooks and springs.

The spring can accomplish all that the well cannot. The well tends to be rather austere and solitary. The spring gushes forth with overt invitations; it feels free to run in any direction. The path is at times unpleasant. It might get sidetracked or polluted, or meet an unexpected bed of sand and run dry. It may travel so far that it loses touch with its source. But these are only occasional incidents which cannot affect its inherent resolve to cover its designated distance.

We are those springs. We are like poets who achieve an awareness of their knowledge in the midst of their speech and are the first ones to be surprised by what they express. Yet for the orator who attempts to speak with such spontaneity, there is always the risk that he will miss the mark. But the audience gives him enough chances. It used to be vain to want to appear in public and humble to hide. Now, as we totter between decline and redemption, we all have the chance to humble ourselves by speaking out; or become impossibly vain if all we want to do is hide.

But not all scholars and teachers acquire the ability to share in proportion to what they possess, and even less are amenable to handing out a portion to those who need it most. When, for whatever reason, they decide to go out in the world, their unseasoned teachings may have a tendency to inhibit the will of those naturally inclined to perpetuate the spring. Such teachings are our Law; they serve to deter ignorance, help decide what is pure or impure, measure the distance between heaven and earth, fix the calendar and figure out the exact cycle of the moon, if not the hour of redemption. Though they were meant to be taught primarily in the houses of study, they would eventually descend to the streets. Such a wonder was only able to be achieved by the Baal Shem Tov's teachings, which would coexist with the profane and not be soiled.

Yet at first these teachings met with resistance from scholars who thought it dangerous because they were too holy to be handed out so freely. Perhaps they thought that it was too early for the world to be redeemed. Some even went so far as to imagine the worst: that they were faced with heresy. The truth is that those teachings were hewn so that whoever humbly placed himself in the right spot would be able to receive them. This design alone made their adherents different from the rest; the teachers' words took on the characteristics of softness and grace, even when issuing a rebuke.

It was evident that, as at Sinai, such a way of learning *Torah* was nourishing the whole person, not just their head. Beards grew longer and saintly visages began to appear. Besides being mere supplication, prayer turned decisively into an instrument of war against the *evil force*. The fear of Heaven, which had been reduced to an academic sentiment, and therefore occasioned very little organic change, now regained its intended function: to make room for the Divine.

That which most offended the opponents of the Baal Shem Tov was their fear that they might possibly be enchanted by his teachings. They knew them to be true, but had neither the soulful ability nor the courage to take the leap. And so they stuck to their old means and forbade themselves and others the usage of this most potent medicine for the soul, by then known as Hasidut.

Kabbalah—the esoteric aspect of Scripture and the ancient parent of Hasidut—had also come at a crucial time to lend vigor to the spring, and it had been equally rebuffed. It had been met with the same tenacious resistance, because scholars of that period adhered to the belief that in order to tackle such holy doctrine one had to be forty years old and erudite in all exoteric study. Therefore, students were warned not to come near that body of work, lest they lose their minds. However, this became law only among the Jews of Eastern Europe, the *Ashkenazim*, but not for their Oriental counterparts, the *Sephardim*. Rather, the Sephardim had turned to the *Zohar*—the seminal book of all Kabbalistic study, an esoteric commentary on the Torah—for spiritual strength. They read it like Psalms and suffered no harm.

The Hasidim and the Sephardim kept in close touch, if not always through direct contact at least in spirit. They were both clear on their respective roles. The Sephardim were the Kabbalists, a magnanimous well, and the Hasidim were running springs. The latter would seek out the former for confirmation of their own discoveries, going either to the Sephardi masters or reading their commentaries. The partnership was ideal. Hasidut would make forays into every exiled land, and Kabbalah would supply it with all the necessary charts. Dig the canals and the Kabbalah would supply the waters. All at once, the Hasidim became the new carriers of esoteric study. Kabbalah had surreptitiously entered their bones via Hasidut. Kabbalistic studies are teachings whose express purpose is to redeem, in that they seep into dry knowledge to make it sweet. They enliven unused study, flatten vanity, give direction, and fill the spirit to satiety.

If Kabbalah, essentially a mystical configuration of Creation, is the mother, then Hasidut is her child. Nothing in the Kabbalah's austere countenance could betray the fact that throughout the centuries she had been smuggling a yet more prodigious form of teaching, one which could only be revealed at a specific time in history, a time when darkness would be at its most dense.

The Hasid, the child of Kabbalah, has his mother's traits and grace, but not her poise, since years of serving in the field have influenced his demeanor. His dark clothing gathers more light than a thousand suns. Yet he is modest enough not to pay attention to how much light he retains, nor would he make an inappropriate display. His fullness is more evident when he is off guard, when he sings or tells stories, or when he dances, when his figure liberates a human current which charges the air. This occurs to the extent that when you join in the dance with other Hasidim, you are carried away by the flow of a human exhalation which binds your bodies into one unified ensemble.

The dance area is packed with precious wisdom that the dancers collect through their dynamic movements. The more participants and the greater the heat, the more potent is the transmission of the mystic knowledge. When the joy is so great that the dancing lasts an entire night, these ambient teachings pour into the street to touch everyone's mind.

Now you may observe that in the streets nothing seems to have changed. Not every mouth can spell out these teachings and not every face can reflect them, even less so the serious face. The inauspiciously serious face, with its ill-timed, irrelevant advertisement for knowledge, is an aggravated version of the human image that is bound to prevent the teaching from spreading. Accordingly, it ought to be considered a crime to wear such a face. If intellect cannot command an honest smile, what type of good is its owner contributing to the world? For a good face helps bring forgotten knowledge to the surface, whereas a stony face buries it. Therefore, one of the great favors one could do for humanity would be to shatter such a hideous mask with laughter. Nothing is as effective. This, in actual fact, is the consummate moment of encounter between spirit and form, where spirit comes humbly as laughter to conquer defiant form, and when the creation of a new being could actually occur through one quick alteration of the face. But this does not come about without occasioning rather painful facial distortions moments before the hide bursts to disclose kinder features. The soul takes an immense pleasure in participating in such a revival. When it is done correctly, with spontaneity and honesty, it cannot but succeed. In this instance, the risk bears a vitalizing wisdom. The end result is akin to the creation of life itself.

Let me relate from my own experience how this works. The most vivid example happened during a talk I gave in Boston. We were in a large room filled with about seventy people, most of them sitting on the carpeted floor. A serious-looking man sat in the first row directly opposite me, stiff and erect, wearing wire rim glasses, and dressed in a white muslin Indian shirt. He was an intellectual collector. He may have been the instructor of a New Age discipline of some sort, but certainly his was an extreme case of a condition that is all too common, where the head finds it increasingly difficult to speak through the heart. You could tell that his heart, having been neglected, had dried up from disuse. As such, it could no longer challenge the mind to excel. This lack of nourishment being exchanged between blood and intellect created a disastrous result: the face was without expression. I made him my point of focus because he gathered within himself everyone else's angst.

Actually, when I first saw him, I was quite impressed. He fairly floated into the room, accompanied by an entourage of young people. And yet, you had only to take a quick look at him to see that despite his glowing appearance, deep down he was a very sad and broken person. The texture and stillness of his face betrayed the fact that he had not laughed in years. As I spoke, he exerted himself to meditate, eyes closed, his head erect. Then it hit me that his bliss was forced. My words could not possibly have warranted the state of trance he assumed. It was unbearable to see him struggle thus on my account. The only thing that I could think of to get him out of his pitiful state was to drop my subject and surprise him with something outrageous. First, I made a facetious remark about the "true believer" syndrome and followed that with a bit of impromptu theatrics, performing an impersonation of a modern day pundit. All of us in the room were laughing except him, and it wasn't for lack of trying. He was really making a valiant effort.

I remember exactly how it happened. First, he had several convulsions in his chest, followed by a stupefied look in his eyes and a jerky, rippling movement across his frozen face. He then placed his palms on the floor in anticipation of something terrible that was about to occur. Fear struck him, and his skin started to crack as petrified muscles suddenly awoke. His face turned a dangerous red, and he let out a raucous, gurgling shriek like a prehistoric beast trying to imitate human laughter. In one breath he roared and cried, rattling on with a weird, unending, "Haw, haw, haw." Then guilt overtook me. He had to be stopped lest he suffer cardiac arrest. But he kept on chortling, even after I tried shifting back to my original subject. Then finally his guffawing ceased, and his skin slowly returned to its original color.

He removed his glasses to wipe them off, then put them back on, and looked at me straight in the eye. I obliged his demand for eye contact as long as he willed it. Only after I left him to pay attention to the rest of the audience did I sense a well of energy rise up to my temples. I felt feverish. The exchange had left me renewed and humbled. He had so affected me, that when I resumed speaking, I did so effortlessly. There was not the slightest trace of didacticism in my words. Inspiration came easily. The intensity with which the audience listened was so tangible that I could literally hear it. It enabled me to articulate with inconceivable ease whatever thought came to mind. I suddenly found myself facing the most receptive vessels, and all that thanks to the laughing man.

ON THE CREATION of the world through successive degrees of revelations, called *vessels*. * The *vessels* break. They endure decline after decline, until they become rubble and stone, because they were selfish. * Emergence of individuals who worship the rubble. * Emergence of the man of faith. This one is an editor who comes up with the sum of the parts, to make contact with the Divine. * On how intellect turns to idol worship. * On how a cold heart and a cold intellect disfigure a face so much as to create an idol. * On diminishing one's presence, thinning the air until divine reality outshines the false beauty of the idol.

Breaking The Vessels

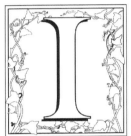T IS WRITTEN in Kabbalistic literature that the world was created through divine manifestations, successive degrees of revelation, which represent divinity in such a way that we can begin to have some grasp of the Infinite. These manifestations, which are referred to as luminaries, or vessels, can be thought of as intermediaries but are a reflection of divinity itself, humbly containing its light to facilitate a transmission. In the same way a person condenses his knowledge to express his ideas to those of lesser understanding, these celestial stations are able to speak to us intelligibly about the divine.

Our holy books explain that when the divine light emanated from the Source and penetrated the vessels to fill them, these vessels shattered into a multitude of fragments which fell down and were lost in this physical universe. It was actually through these stations, that this material world was created. In describing how the vessels broke, our sages comment that they could not withstand the magnitude of the light, and that this was because there was no harmony among them. Each vessel was distant from and independent of its neighbor. They were like selfish individuals who live their own lives and have no love for one another.

The fragments that remained after the fall endured decline after decline, materializing even into stone. As people came along and began cementing the rubble, erecting cities, paving roads and carving statues, every available spark of light became entrapped inside the thick walls of darkness.

Our world is a beautiful place. Who would not be mesmerized by its enchanting *tableaux*? Rolling hills, dotted with tiny white homes, are nests that house the blue of heaven. Small towns stretch out along the rivers, among the shifting greens of the valleys. A sweet singer's voice wafts in the dry heat of a summer afternoon and as night obscures the scarlet horizon with swift brush strokes of black, a man sits rocking on his porch, pulling on an old briar pipe. Everything seems to be in good order, though it may turn out to be nothing more than organized debris, a fragile assemblage. Suddenly, in the eye of the beholder, this entire world can revert to a howling nightmare of illusion; it may be triggered by a dream, a vision, a failure in business or a death in the family. Once our tenuous notion of reality is shattered, we will deny our lifeblood; curse the day we were born and the breast that nurtured us. Confused, we seek refuge in a number of contrived methods that offer some shred of meaning in the midst of our wanderings. Finally, we find shelter in a forced and artificial harmony and survive at the outskirts of entropy. We become patients in the care of therapists who are too short of breath to stir their clients' souls, who have too little life within themselves to inspire others to thrive. So we cope, with breezy conversation and letting go of rage. One gains a sort of wisdom, the kind convalescents acquire during their years of combat with disease. The spirit is gone, paved over by the cure. Now insulated, we opt for a life filled with those small treasures that make life worth living. There is no flight, no dance of the soul, no chance to shift into overdrive and link our earthly existence with its heavenly Source.

I would rather not be the bearer of bad news, but our world has hit rock bottom. Our sphere of existence cannot descend any lower than where it is now. The great voyage has already happened. We have arrived. But this does not preclude the possibility of further decline within the individual's sphere of existence, where every blunder is patterned after the primordial fall.

History has shown that people have been demonstrating two basically different attitudes after the primordial fall. There are those who, after judging the voyage to be impossible, learn to satisfy themselves with whatever they possess in the pits, and there are those who will use every means at their disposal to return to the Source. In their search for some type of spiritual gratification, the former have been known to have a tendency toward idol worship; whereas, by contrast, the latter essentially use biblical texts, believing in one governing Supreme Being. If the former activate their worship with personal ideas and images, the latter do so with the *mitzvah*, the deed, whose nature is to connect its doer with the Source.

So here are two people. One dabbles in idol worship and the other is a man of faith. Whatever gets the former through the night is good enough for him. He will go as far as finding power in fragments of wood, metal, or crystal, as long as it moves him. He has nothing but his own mind to organize his worship. He does not hesitate to build his spiritual capital on half-baked ideas. What he wants most is to unpack, warm his bones, and belong someplace.

The latter, on the other hand, would rather die than bow to scraps and shards. His method is that of an editor. He cannot settle for fragments of truth taken out of context. He puts pieces together, sifting through everything he finds, until, after years of tests and trials, he comes up with the sum of the parts, a wholesomeness that leads him directly to the Divine. He will not kneel until the revelation is complete.

In that sense, one can easily conceive how an "intellectual", someone who lives most of his life in his head, could possibly fall into the first category: an idol worshipper. For he lacks the sort of warmth only the heart can procure, fusing events coming from different directions, or realities, into one harmonious whole. In other words, he is not adept at reading the working of Divine Providence. He cannot conceive that all contacts between the abstract and the tangible, between the gift and the vessel, are matches willed by Heaven.

He finds it difficult to believe that the meeting of a fish and a passing fly it feeds on is an event that has been orchestrated from Above. The same is true for every rolling stone and the spot where it comes to rest, or for every fluent thought in the mind where it occurs. Each of these otherwise unforeseen unions dare the intellect to probe more deeply into the divine purpose. They serve as evidence that it is Heaven's hand which moves the four winds, creates the rain, and cracks open the seed, which in turn provides the bed-ridden with the proper cure, or through some carefully staged incident, goads the criminal mind to a change of direction.

I would not go as far as labeling the bearer of such an undiscerning mind an idol worshipper, but he is close. His service to the idol is not altogether conscious, and may never be, because his idol is not one with a defined form. This idol dwells mainly in thought. This one grows in direct proportion to how much a person's heart is cold. The intellect may be uncommonly great, but somehow it is inadequate to warm the heart, which activates love. And if it is so, if intellect cannot put itself in the service of love, it will of necessity have to find an outlet to discharge excess steam. It will debate. And it will hurt. Its decisions will be partial, because only one fragment of the person is making them. It is a hired gun which is only geared to win. Anger, which deforms the face, is usually common in such a type of intellect, all of which is enough proof that the power of intelligence is idolatry indeed.

What the bearer of such an intellect ought to do is present his idol to a designated place of reality, where spirit and form meet in a superlative manner; namely, before the *Tzaddik*, the Just, and there shatter the idol. This would, at the same time, be the quickest manner for acquainting himself with the workings of Divine Providence. The awakening to such reality, where form and spirit coexist in such a manner as to speak directly to the soul, is bound to occur, in view of the fact that the eyes of the *Tzaddik* have never gazed upon evil sceneries, that his hands have never selfishly grabbed even the most legitimate of pleasures, and that his tongue has never ventured to search for sensational tastes. Best of all, he has never thought ill of anyone. It will suffice to look at his translucent skin to be convinced that his body is as holy as his thoughts are pure.

Every *mitzvah* that a *Tzaddik* performs must absorb the sacred like a sponge. Otherwise, what is it that gives him such a seraphic appearance? Most of us, on the other hand, are rather mental in the sense that we do not practice half of the deeds that we have engaged ourselves to observe. We are liars, in that we command more attention with our mouths than with our actions, but it is not possible to extend our fakery for very long. Fortunately, our somber faces put a stop to it all. In extreme cases, our bodies are compelled to disprove the excellence of our speech. The flesh will always be there to refute thought's allegation that it has already come to see the light. In the worst cases, when very few really good deeds exist to ease their encounter, form and spirit so reject one another that adverse repercussions arise, creating distortions in behavior, as is the case with the preacher's tragicomic stance, his affected grace and mock piety, his clean-shaven, less than sanguine face, his illuminated eyes stuck in a visionless gaze, and his state of bliss framed by tense jaws or betrayed by a sullen demeanor. All of these provide providential information as to the person's true status. Regardless of the claim it makes, such base intellect cannot possibly discern the sacred, even less so advertise it.

As for the primitive forms of idol worship, they have sharply declined, but their stereotype is still prevalent. Those complacent smiles on petrified icons can still have an uncanny effect on the psyche. In some parts of the world they still do, but generally speaking, they have lost much of their power over the human spirit. Having done their time, many of them are now stored in dark cellars along with other debris. The lucky ones get a pedestal in a museum. Their sad marble eyes seem to stare at those bygone days when pilgrims came in droves, laden with all manner of offerings. In their time, they were feared. Best of all was the fun they had challenging the Jews.

But now who is filling their shoes? No one, not really. Yet idolatry has managed to go through a revolution in form. A statue is not necessarily required. The old guard has given way to more mercurial gods, newcomers who assume an abstract appearance and spare us the prostrations. Sometimes they do take on a more visible form. Money holds a powerful sway over its adorers. Have you ever looked into the eyes of a miser who is counting his fortune? Have you ever observed the tenderness with which his fingers handle the wads of bills? It is difficult to decide which procures the greater ecstasy, the physical manipulation of hard cash, or the cool contemplation of a fortune that is somewhere safely stashed away. Any way you look at it, money is the universal idol, flagrantly worshipped by too many, regardless of race, color, or creed. People feed on the visions of things they would like to buy, but cannot, so they caress them with their eyes by day and own them in their sleep. And do not think this longing is any less for those who have already acquired material wealth. In their case, the worshipping is not so frenetic. It is somewhat passive, if not serene.

As far as the not so discernible forms of strange worship are concerned, secularized and quasi spiritual systems are having a field day, especially during the past three decades, defining existence and selling their concept of it at prohibitive prices. The idol often consists of a potpourri of Eastern and Western ideologies smartly assembled to conform to the amalgam of fragments that constitute modern man.

The techniques generally aim at self improvement and the restructuring of those fragments. The restructuring, however, can never be complete or real, because Heaven is denied a substantial role in the endeavor. Honesty, which these systems invariably promote, becomes diseased from excessive use. It is there to work only as a therapy, a mere protective exercise of the psyche. This psyche now exists reconditioned and repackaged as a commodity. It is trained to think and act positively. All that matters is that things get done, regardless of the fact that the motivation is utterly artificial. Self evaluation as well as any moral or ethical standards are discarded in lieu of peremptory dogma. Love is no love. Laughter is no laughter. True joy is never experienced. Spiritual subsistence is mainly obtained through precise but shallow definitions, not through wisdom or faith. The resilient independence which these burgeoning movements afford their adherents is a false certainty that has overtones of arrogance. Their lack of humility lends them faces that do not transmit divinity. Their style is sentimental, often childish, yet they abhor sentimentality. The pleasure of existence is all theirs. They share none of it with the heavens. They generally do not fail in business, yet find it hard to give charity in a way that redeems life. Such a prospect generally disgusts them. They keep compassion on a leash. Their love for the neighbor is more or less perfunctory.

But these new modes of worship are mild stuff compared to the old idolatry. They only look so dreadful to us now because we have lost the perspective with which to accurately evaluate the magnitude of their flaws. There is definitely a touch of evil here, but not as much as our fears have led us to believe. Those enmeshed in any of them are sincerely looking for answers. They have indeed found some and are daring us to do at least as well. The problem is: Who is there that is so genuinely spirited and lively that could display a truer life before them, doing so with no additional words or contrived axioms and adding no further definitions?

Who will bring effervescent life running to and fro before their eyes, rendering them dizzy with authentic joy?

The key, I believe, is to make ourselves lighter, less thick, more apt to transmit divine light. The weight of cynicism and pretense would have to be cast off. Instead, we should show our true faces. In brief, we owe it to Heaven to give of ourselves, to such an extent that we disappear a bit. The idea is to come to a point that we diminish our presence in such a manner as to thin the air, to the point that the divine reality outshines the false beauty of the idol.

5

ON THE DISAPPEARANCE of the small man in the big world, following the story of a poor Spanish soldier who is coerced to cede his place to a rich man, as they are both waiting for tickets in the train station in Madrid. * On the spiritual descent of a prominent family. * God makes room to create the world. * The true teacher uses small speech, disappears a bit to make room for the student's growth. * Comparing an empty mind to an empty room, given to mad winds. * Breaking the wall that divides the two halves of the heart, to create one large room, to make love less selective. * On changing darkness into light, and repairing the vessels.

MAKING ROOM

HE IDEA OF making room has been with me for as long as I can remember. I was, however, to become truly conscious of it only after an incident that occurred in Spain. For years it had been my wish to visit the country where my ancestors had lived some five hundred years earlier, before the Inquisition chased them out. I had arrived the previous day, and had spent the night in a small hotel. In the morning I took a long stroll to view the city. It struck me, during those few hours, how most people's faces looked familiar. I came across hundreds of cousins. The resemblance was so great that I frequently had to restrain myself from greeting perfect strangers. I felt very much at home, and was enjoying the feeling immensely.

It was with that exhilarated spirit that I entered the Madrid railroad station in the afternoon. I was on my way to a small village in the *Costa del Sol*, where I hoped to recuperate from a recent illness. The station was swarming with people. I stood in line behind a soldier in green fatigues.

A few yards to the right of the line stood a policeman, his rifle hanging heavily from his shoulder, an ammunition belt slung across his chest and the hard black hat of the

Spanish Military Police tilting down across his brow over beads of sweat. Behind him, walking toward us, was a man in his forties with well-oiled hair combed neatly back. The impeccable trim of his mustache and the soft leather of his shoes could only have belonged to a man of money and class. He stood at ease, holding a newspaper in front of his face. He took a quick look at the line and came to stand behind me, still reading.

The policeman assessed the situation cooly, walked towards the soldier and motioned with his hand as if to say, "What are you doing here? Can't you see who is behind you?" After a glance at the expanse of newspaper behind which that mustachioed head was still buried, the soldier shriveled, bent to pick up his duffel bag and stepped quickly out of the line. The policeman helped him along with a pinch and a pull on the collar of his shirt. Then, with a flourish, he guided the rich man, who was still one with his newspaper, to his rightful place in line. The soldier stood off to the side, his face red with shame, accepting the affront as if it was his due.

I was seething, to say the least, and could not decide upon whom to unleash my fury first: the policeman for his officiousness; or the greasy head now in front of me for his heartlessness; or the little soldier, for being so quick to swallow his pride and failing to respond to the insult. But I held my peace. In those days, in Franco's Spain, the slightest hint of revolt would have branded you a menace to society and you might easily have rotted in some remote prison for the rest of your days. I was not about to die a hero on foreign soil. I decided it would be wise to appease my mind with less perilous thoughts.

It did not take long to adjust my thoughts concerning the arrogant policeman. Without his rifle and intimidating uniform, he would have surely been another person. I pictured him sitting at a café with friends, men like him, country folk who had come to the city to make their way. I imagined him relaxing and telling a few jokes, perhaps speaking in proverbs as Spaniards often do. He soon became so different from the way the system had cast him, that my disgust for him disappeared.

As for the rich man, I had only the nape of his neck before my eyes. I would need to have a better look if I were to see whether he too could be redeemed. He must have read my mind, for he shifted slightly to the right and turned to look at me, tilting his head and greeting me with a smile. I surprised myself by returning the courtesy and noticed that he looked very much like an uncle of mine. I took a liking to him just because of that. The man went back to his reading.

I then began to stare at the soldier, now moving sheepishly towards the end of the line. He eyed me suspiciously, as though afraid that I was in league with the authorities, and made himself appear meeker than he really was. My immediate response was to put him at ease with the most genuine and affable composure I could muster. Gratefully, he bowed his head three times in rapid succession. Concealed behind that mincing, ingratiating gesture, I saw the stature of one who in his own home must no doubt be his own person. I inclined my head once, in a lordly manner, to lend his bows the mark of kingship he deserved. That encouraged him to walk with surer steps toward the end of the queue.

Throughout my years, that soldier in fatigues has popped up in other places, in different garb. The characters and settings may vary, but whenever "little" men meet with the "high and mighty," the plot and its outcome are likely to be the same. Viewed from a distance, it seems a strangely choreographed spectacle, in which the actors never manage to meet face to face. The "little" man appears poised and important as he prepares to venture forth from his private world. As soon as he steps out into the street, half of his majesty has faded away and, on encountering his antagonist, he is suddenly stripped of every shred of his dignity. It happens automatically, without argument, as if by some inexorable chemistry. Not one word is said, no contact is made. The little man fears to lift his head while on the big man's turf, whereas the latter is as oblivious to the former's presence as he is to his own arrogance. Perfunctorily, he turns to some other concern, unaware that he has obliterated his brother.

The oppression of the small by the powerful, egocentric people prompts men of social conscience to rise up and preach esteem for and to the weak. Their goal is to provide the disadvantaged with the means to defend themselves against the elite. To give vent to their ideas, ideologues hire able choreographers to stage a new production about oppression, starring the same little soldier in fatigues. In the opening scene they have him leaving his home, stalwart and commanding respect. As the play unfolds, he is gradually stripped of his identity. He is hardly noticed by anyone, including the oppressed themselves, and he gradually falls into a deep depression. He is no longer king in his own house. By this time, there is not one spectator in the audience with a dry eye. Things go from bad to worse until a wind of revolt comes to change the order of things. Miraculously, no one is hurt. Everything ends well. The oppressed mingle freely with their former oppressors. Peace is celebrated with dances in the streets. The audience exalts in rapture over the flawless execution of the troupe, and at the grand finale all the actors come forward as one, with arms outstretched, throwing kisses to the crowd. The loudest bravos come from the well to do.

Even the critics are pleased. All, except one. While the audience mills about in the lobby and heads for the exits, he remains in his seat, scribbling his last few impressions of the evening, then hurries out a side door to meet his deadline. His morning review creates quite a stir, for it is the only unfavorable notice the play has received. The audience was handily seduced, he says. When carefully analyzed, the show amounts to not much more than a mélange of paper-thin feelings. There were no true relationships between the people, only emotional outbursts and shallow regrets. The damages were too quickly repaired, hastily stitched, and ironed smooth with sophisticated grimaces and politeness. His critique continues with a few words of praise for the actors' faithful renditions and for the producers' concern for the little man's cause. The script, he bemoans, has betrayed a superficial sense of justice, and the poor soldier has lost his soul in the process. The critic sardonically excuses the playwright for failing to convey any meaning to the notion of making room for the small. The playwright, after all, is the product of his time. All things considered, he cannot be expected to have done any better. What one cannot understand, one can only fake. That, he concludes, was the upshot of the evening:

spurious action and forced responses on both sides of the proscenium arch. Whatever success the playwright might have will be due to the fortuitous match of well-staged cosmetic sentiments with the scant compassion that audiences are willing to spare in their off-hours, all of which points to the world's lack of love.

It would seem that the critic is one of those few Just ones on whom the world stands, but he is not. He is a good man, by all means. Playwrights have come to fear him, to the point that they frequently compose their works for commercial purposes in compliance with his rather staunch ideals. What no one knows, however, is that the man is hopelessly lonely. He and his wife now sleep in separate rooms. His children left home as soon as they could afford to. With his role so whittled down, he could not be better qualified to lament the loss of love. His usefulness, however, ends there.

In his diminished state, he is expert only at pointing out deficiencies, rarely at correcting them. He can, for example, spot those empty embraces where only bodies meet. He can read the rupture between two souls, and he knows how much of a person dies in a bad relationship. In a way, he is a prophet of his time. The only trouble is that he does not have shoulders broad enough to carry his ideals. A tragic figure, indeed, but there is more to this story. This is, after all, an epic tragedy.

As a child in Lithuania, the critic had a grandfather who would take him on his knee and delight his young mind with tales of long-forgotten times. The stories sometimes contained concepts that only an adult could understand, but they were so simply and skillfully told that the boy still reaped both pleasure and profit. The one he remembers most vividly was told a few days before his grandfather died. They were alone in the room. The old man had gotten out of bed with great difficulty and sat on a chair so as not to perturb the child. He took him on his lap and began one last story, into which was woven one last bit of advice for future years.

"This world below," the old man had said, "was meant to be a place for people to meet. These meetings are our chance to gather the knowledge and the strength to fly back up to heaven. Every person is like a kind of traveling light, looking for company in this dark world. When two lights come together, the success of their journey will depend on how much each traveler is willing to give. The best possible result, when two lights meet, is the birth of a third light. It might be very small, not nearly as bright as the other two, but it is strong enough to command them to forget their size and to convince them to live together in peace. For your mother and father, you are that light, and even though they are bigger than you, your light shines much more brightly."

"That," the grandfather went on to say, "is what happens when two good people meet and a boy like you is born. But if, heaven forbid, two hardheaded people come together and refuse to dim their lights for each other, all they will create is darkness. In fact, that is how chaos began in the world, with vessels of light fighting over trifles, until they finally collapsed and shattered. Therefore, my child, you who are as dear to me as my own soul, remember, as you grow, not to make hasty judgments about people you will meet. Do your best to make all their lights shine. Always strive to make room in your world for others to exist. This, in brief, is everything our Scriptures mean to teach." The old man then kissed and blessed his grandchild, and sent him scurrying out to play.

As thinking men are apt to do in the declining days of their lives, the aging critic is given lately to rumination. In one such nostalgic reverie, he recalls the time he was awarded the title of Philosopher Emeritus by the National Society for the Preservation of Humankind. His eldest grandson, age nineteen, had taken a few days off from his sophomore year of school to attend the affair. Everyone in the family agreed that he was the one most likely to perpetuate the old man's concern and verve. After the presentation ceremony, the two of them sat together and talked late into the night. In the course of the conversation, the old man gave over as faithful a version as he could of his own grandfather's last advice. There was an important difference, however. Lacking a background in the holy teachings, yet eager to make the point, the critic filled his tale with eclectic references to the poets, playwrights, and metaphysicians of every era in whose writings he found parallels to the wisdom he had heard as a child.

The young man listened well enough. Upon returning to university, he began to discover solid correlates in the teachings of one contemporary pundit in particular. Among the maxims of this latter day seer was the idea that every person needs his space. That seemed to him to approximate his ancestor's creed. Towards the end of his second year in graduate school, his grandfather passed away, with a verse of Shakespeare on his lips. Soon the gifted young man began to spread his teacher's gospel.

He took it upon himself to disseminate his newly found knowledge by giving numerous lectures and workshops. For these, he advertised vigorously, postering the city and distributing pamphlets at malls and busy intersections. He was prone at times to fits of nervous exhaustion, but usually managed to stop short of total collapse by using progressive relaxation techniques. At the age of twenty-six, he left his teacher, got married, and opened a school, which quickly earned him a good income. Pressure began to get to him, however, and before long he suffered a severe nervous breakdown, which he treated with a combination of drugs and deep breathing.

The couple gave birth to a baby boy and named him after his late great grandfather, the critic. The room they gave him was rather large for a child of that age. It was twenty by twenty-four feet, overlooking an elegant park. They painted the walls sky blue, to effect a sort of heavenly nest. The little boy lived there in solitude, for he was given no brothers or sisters. More than once he would wake up screaming after nightmares in which he felt himself falling through endless space. On the advice of a prominent child psychologist his parents decided never to hold him and thus foster his independence. Slowly, there emerged a subtle split in his personality, a dual addiction to being both held and left alone. He received exactly one hug and one kiss on each of his birthdays.

Eventually, he learned to utilize the intelligence that ran in the family and managed to explain away his aberrations with a perverse philosophical finesse. He took advantage of his situation by commercializing those aberrations. He wrote novels which became instant bestsellers. Later on, he switched to films in which he psychoanalyzed himself by discharging his neuroses on the screen. He wrote and directed almost one film each year, on the advice of his therapist, and he grew healthier as a result. He promised to get married by the end of his twentieth film, and so he did. While the priest and the rabbi, who together performed the wedding ceremony, quoted lines out of old movies, a chamber orchestra played serial music. Either out of guilt, or perhaps out of a sincere heart, when he and the bride were still under the canopy, he pledged to plant one hundred trees in the Galilee. The bareheaded rabbi was so thrilled by the announcement that he grabbed the microphone and delivered a partisan Israeli song in a superb baritone voice. Right after that, everyone held hands and danced the *hora*. Jews around the world felt proud when they were informed of the movie director's gift to Israel. The headline of a weekly tabloid read "Movie Mogul Pledges Planting of Entire Forest."

B efore creation, until that ungraspable event we call "The Beginning", there was neither time nor space, neither past nor future, there was no north, south, east or west, no heavens above and nothing beneath. There was not a clue in that unfathomable expanse to hint at the impending formation of planetary systems, much less at the embodiment of the human design. Our holy books reveal that there was but radiant, limitless light permeating the boundless, until the Creator withdrew Himself, so to speak, to create a void, a dimension within the dimensionless, in which life could possibly take form.

In a similar vein, every creation is, of necessity, preceded by the initial action of making room. To choose a classic example, the creative process occurs between teacher and disciple, where the teacher's main function is to see to it that he does not stultify the growth of his disciple with his own brilliance. Brilliant teaching does very little to build the person. It may touch the mind, but has very little effect on the flesh. By contrast, true intelligence, which is an overt expression of the soul, can speak to the whole person. It goes through myriad contractions before it uses small speech. With small speech, it is able to influence the body, like a horse is influenced by the command of its rider. As opposed to brilliance, which mostly serves to thicken the ego, intelligence thins out the flesh. The thinning out causes the one providing the teaching to disappear a bit, to make himself so light as to allow the listener to develop his own vision of the invisible infinite. The teacher is there and not there, both assertive and self-effacing. He has the good sense to know when to advance and when to retreat. A few humorous remarks will serve to make him quasi invisible. The laughter that those remarks provoke open up the bodily conduits to make room for deeper understanding. It foments a small revolution in the cerebrum, before it fills it with redemptive knowledge. Such an organized chaos, as it were, prepares one for renewed growth. All the while, God is present, because the transparent face of the teacher does not block Him.

R ecently, a group of friends were gathered in my home on Saturday night. For a moment, the conversation took a somber turn as we spoke of how many people seem so fragile, on the verge of falling apart, and how, in their helplessness, they turn to us when we ourselves are struggling to hold our ground. We were reminded of another occasion, years ago, when we had grown anxious over the sudden illness of the Moses of our generation, the Lubavitcher Rebbe. Someone remarked that the Rebbe had, in fact, done us a favor by falling ill. He had made room for us to come into our own, withdrew for a while to let us make full use of faculties which might otherwise have remained undeveloped. In his temporary absence he had made us more mindful of the urgency of our tasks. Someone else spoke of how, in crises, we are able to do the impossible, and at some time in our lives, we have performed beyond our aptitudes in unfamiliar fields, or witnessed our shortcomings being steamrolled by our determination to succeed. Another recounted how, in our long history, we have waged war and prevailed against all odds, outnumbered a hundred to one.

We also spoke about the different ways to eradicate despair, the worst of all spiritual afflictions. Despair cancels the reasoning powers of memory and empties the mind of past certitudes. We took off on the idea of how an empty mind is like an empty room with open doors and windows, given to mad winds. The winds whistle in such a mind. We also spoke of how too long an exposure to such winds can result in a loss of identity. We debated the most expedient way to avoid such permanent injury.

It was getting late, but we kept at it, exchanging outrageous strategies. We decided that before anything else, we were going to rekindle the *dead hearts*, our own first. We were going to bang our heads against the hard wall of our divided heart until we could unite its two halves into one large chamber, if we wanted our heart to include the multitude. We imagined ways to break that hard wall where love and hatred are simultaneously and distinctively expressed in the space of the same beat.

We were going to give love new dimensions. By uniting the two halves, our love for others would become less selective; we would be inclined to love others, not only our kin. The fringe benefit of all that would be that the want of pleasure would have a lighter grip on our thinking. Pleasure would not necessarily be the exclusive quantum unit of life. Greed, a morbid capitalization of pleasure, would no longer occupy every single moment. Subsequently, people would live more meaningful lives. We each advanced a different slant, to bring the dividing walls down. One offered to sing. One said he would dance. A third volunteered to bark. Two friends proposed to go on a hunger strike and carry signs. Then one, who had remained silent throughout the evening, submitted his opinion that no one single plan would suffice. He announced that he would strive, for the sake of the cause, and at the risk of becoming unhinged, to do all of the above at once. This rather ambitious suggestion prompted me to pronounce, in a somewhat less facetious tone, the epitaph of the era of specialization. I proceeded to wrest a pledge from all of those present to turn into jacks of all trades. We would knock on our scholars' and rabbis' doors and beg them to come down into the street to do the same. We would each become responsible for whatever problems came our way and never again pass the buck. We would squarely face those who came in need of rest or rejuvenation, and give it on the spot. On that note, we finally parted company, promising one another, as we stood by the door, to have more such Saturday night meetings.

L ate that night, after my friends had left, I was too agitated to go to bed. I sat at my desk until dawn, struggling to describe in words what we had achieved with our mere presence. We had changed darkness into light. Yet, my words were powerless to demonstrate what I had seen happen moments earlier. I felt deep frustration when I finally went to bed. In the morning, as I awoke, I gave it another try. I was giving up hope when, auspiciously, my thoughts turned to a story about our great sage, Rabbi Shimon Bar Yohai, the author of the Zohar. Rabbi Shimon's disciple, Rabbi Chiya, was about to enter his teacher's chamber along with some fellow students, when suddenly they heard a voice that called out, "Which of you, before coming here, has changed darkness into light, and bitter into sweet? Otherwise, do not approach here!" The answer came back that Rabbi Chiya had indeed done so. Upon hearing that, Rabbi Shimon ordered that Rabbi Chiya be permitted to enter without further delay.

The story so affected me when I first heard it, that for years it left me imagining how the change from darkness to light could be achieved. I tended to believe it was done through secret formulae. I imagined mighty wizards grabbing handfuls of soot and moments later opening their hands to release beams of light which bounced out of their palms, but that early morning it occurred to me that the change did not take place in some occult manner. The change had to take place inside a vessel. Just consider how an electric light is distinguishable to the eye only when it is contained in a light bulb. There, inside the bulb, light takes on a more tangible reality. However, should the bulb break, light is dispersed. This has its parallel in the spiritual realm where people are vessels in constant need of mending. In other words, the fault is mostly with the vessel. The repair happens progressively, as we pick up, one by one, the shattered pieces, but chances are, that as we busy ourselves with the vessels of those in need, these might harbor resentment about our simplified way of doing things. They might want to see the light. They might demand that we implement a higher spiritual standard, but we must proceed with what we know best, namely, preparing the place by collecting the pieces and putting them in order, and not ceasing to do so until the vessel shines.

6

ABOUT A VAIN man who is shaken like an apple tree to free him of his vanity. * On the imperative of freeing a friend from his jail. * On how the guest turns a prison, your house, into a home. * The mystical bond between guest and host, versus the evil impulse and his schemes. * The devil does not like to joke. How he is an invalid and a voyeur. Like the snake, he has lost the ability to taste, which might explain his nasty behavior. * On how the vain are the snake's greatest inspiration to do evil. * On how the Jewish child is taught early in life to discern the subtle manifestations of the dark forces. * Going past the danger zone, thanks to a coin given to charity.

BEYOND THE FRONTIER

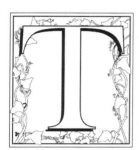HE MAN WHO sat before me was wearing a black coat and a round black hat, and had a full beard with long side curls. Literally half of his body was covered with thick, hard scales. As he described the details of his life, I discovered that he was in his late thirties and married, with several children. He was a scholar who had studied the *Talmud* in *yeshiva* since childhood. The way in which he insisted on repeating that last point several times provided a window through which I began to catch sight of the root of his true malady. I told him that he had likely come to me for some other, less apparent problem, his nerves, perhaps. He kept to his story, repeating that he had no other problem but his skin condition. My experience, however, had taught me to distinguish symptom from disease, so I pressed on, encouraging him to speak out. Finally he conceded that he often suffered from bouts of tension, but, as we sat opposite one another, I began to detect that his problem lay deeper still.

I told him gently that he was possessed with sufficient pride to blow off mountain tops. He didn't like that a bit, but managed to remain composed enough to ask me how I had come to that conclusion. I explained that he sounded like a boiling tea kettle that was about to explode. He smiled uncomfortably, confessing that it was indeed so, but insisting that his condition had passed the point where he was capable of helping himself. As he spoke, he kept his head down. Soon, however, a habitual air of satisfaction eclipsed his momentary state of humility. "What can I possibly do?" he asked, raising his head above me. "I have yet to find someone who can teach Talmud as well as I do!" he declared.

I knew that some people might think that way, but I never heard anyone say it outright. This man had to be given a lesson. Something drastic had to be done. I got up, and without warning, grabbed him by the lapels and shook him vigorously. I felt compelled to do so. How else was I to humble him? Action had to be taken quickly. He was vain, but fortunately his vanity was still at the childish stage. Shaking him, I berated him that his skin disease was a physical manifestation of his pride. Consider what I did as poetic license in the world of action, where extreme behavior serves to make the point. He had gone beyond the limits and that was why the excess oozed through his pores. When I shook him, he had fear in his eyes and had not even really tried to free himself from me, nor had he tried to refute my outrageous diagnosis. The entire episode had lasted for only a few moments.

When I finally released him from my grip he was still dazed. He took a few quick breaths, reclined restfully against the back of his seat, and let out a blusterous exhalation. A quiescent beauty emerged on his face. We then proceeded to chat like old friends before I recommended a diet for him and suggested a combination of herbs for his skin. Our meeting ended with a hug by the door. Walking away, he turned back and winked at me, acknowledging his thanks for my having purged him of his *meshugas*. It is evident that it was only a temporary relief, but it was a first, important breach of his vanity just the same.

You cannot be sure whether this kind of spontaneous intervention is more a function of the rational mind, or an impulse of the will. Perhaps all of the faculties are acting at the same time. The one thing that is certain is that you have to work fast. The door opens just a crack and there is not a second to waste. A weighed decision is already too late. You must plunge head first without worrying whether you will be accepted inside or not. It takes a lot of *chutzpah*, to say the least. It all happens so quickly, the ego is given practically no time to judge or evaluate the situation. There is no room for hurt feelings either. One's worst enemy is fear, which accentuates a lack of faith in ourselves. A lack of faith means a loss of speed. If we miss, we will be taken for mad, but if we succeed, we are redeemers. It works on anyone, even those who are placed above us socially. They are also in desperate need to get out of their jail. They are imprisoned by their false role of ruling over others. Someone has to bring them down by kicking their habit for them, but no one dares. That is precisely what I did with the vain man. Pulling at his coat served only as a means of communicating my concerns. In that instance, it was the right button, the metaphysical acupuncture point of pride.

But take heed, for this rare conduct can only be inspired by the moment. Such a brazen display is not always what is required. Another circumstance would call for very different behavior. One might unleash a funny gesture, in the nature of those feints commonly used with difficult children when parents have to invent all sorts of tricks to divert them from a flare-up of rage. Most of the time, however, a word could be so rich in nuances as to alert all the senses. It would speak directly to the soul.

The faculty of which I am speaking is not an inbred ability, nor is it a psychic power. I would call it a language, one which was once widely spoken but has now fallen into disuse. We did not grow out of it. On the contrary, we happened to no longer be fit for it. It simply flew out of our mouths. Its uncommon speed must have contributed to precipitating its disuse, for it occurs so quickly, it goes unnoticed. Its nature causes it to be easily forgotten, as well as to being misconstrued as fiction, if not folly or scheme. In our time, when empiricism, and its progeny, technology, seem to be the overriding template of our lives, and where the miraculous is discounted or fetishized, empathy is discordant. The proud and the puritan are most inclined to deny the existence of such a faculty because such individuals lack the humor and the humility to condescend to understanding how it works. But, in my mind, what resists it the most is a phobia that people have of anything new, foreign—or ancient.

I acquired this faculty from guests, first in my parents' home and later in my own house. One of the guest's functions is to broaden our knowledge of the world. Through their visitations, they invest us with the means with which we can better understand others, as well as ourselves. They come to ease us of our pressing and unfounded need for privacy. They possess the power to turn a prison into a home. The transaction works both ways. By giving them permission to intrude into our lives, we gain the tacit permission to enter theirs, to free them as they have freed us. The more guests, the more daring our intrusions. Each guest comes to smuggle light into our homes, in the manner that food transfuses its ingrained holy sparks into our system. The more light, the more fluid is our interaction with others. Language, in that instance, is created out of a transubstantiation of our guests. Anthropomorphic form turns into articulate speech. Here creation works in the reverse order. It is a time when the spirit is refueled with provision for those moments when creation resumes its natural course, when our words are able to influence the flesh. Our fate seems to hinge on those mystical changeovers. The problem is, how long can such a tenuous bridge hold? Who will dare to upset the course of that two-way traffic? The odds are that the disturbance will be initiated by a third party, a force which dwells inside all of us, one that we Jews call the *evil inclination*, or *evil impulse*. Its most ingratiating and despicable appellation is the *devil*.

When, at times, I use that latter epithet, it will not be so much because I am particularly obsessed by the character to which it alludes, as I am using it as a literary device to embellish my narrative. Notwithstanding, whatever our personal stand on that may be, we all have to admit that the sole mention of that name still holds a certain sway on the psyche. For isn't the devil responsible for juicing up much of our literature? Even the most skeptical of people ascribe to him a role. My true intent, however, is to demystify him. The least I can accomplish is to produce some evidence about his existential uncertainties. For isn't it we who thicken his reality with our thoughts or deeds? From our misdeeds, he has managed to maintain a thriving business. He owns at least one share in each of us and he is constantly shopping for new opportunities, waiting for the appropriate time when, in a moment of weakness, one of us will let his sentiments or passions be used for purposes not our own. He takes his job seriously. He has no sense of humor, despite the fact that he is one hell of an entertainer.

The reason for his lack of humor can only be explained by the fact that humor can only be borne by a mind which is able to confront both good and evil. He knows only the latter. He stands shrieking in anguish outside the doors of our joyous gatherings, begging the guests not to share in the joy. He hates weddings, circumcisions, and *Bar Mitzvah* parties. His crowning achievement is to break up a marriage or to destroy a friendship.

In spite of his evident power, he himself is vulnerable. He is a product of each generation. He is a hustler, who likes to extend himself to the limit, even if it means that he is occasionally vanquished. He is a chameleon, who adapts himself to our vain desire for quick and easy powers, such as *Ouija* boards, exorcisms, incantations, and other macabre means. Anyone using such tools is quite likely to be subverted by him. Yet, as surely as he enjoys using our services, he really despises anything that is decidedly too cliché in our allegiance to him. He gets nauseated from being portrayed with horns and hooves.

Like the snake in the Garden of Eden, who initially exaggerated the sense of touch and taste to the point of rendering them morbid, he has likewise been cursed for taking pleasure in nothing, neither in the goodness of the earth nor in that of heaven. He is an invalid. He is a voyeur. His frustration over not belonging in either world has him going to extremes. On the one hand, he has the insatiable urge to provoke humans, to wreak havoc on their bodies and souls. On the other hand, he lurks behind the Just, who are the closest entity to heaven. He sits by their gates like a beggar, hoping to catch a glimpse of them. He wants their attention, but they give him none, not even an insult. If he could provoke a curse upon himself, he would consider it a blessing, for it would give him a shot of reality, which he craves. We, however, who are not so complete as the Just, must exercise extreme caution against him, and yet, the irony is that the devil has his weak points. *His* evil inclination is *good*. He cannot explain why that happens to him, but one thing is certain: He never softens his stand in dealings with vain individuals, who most likely are his greatest inspiration to do evil. He enters inside them like the wind. He helps them swing their arms, prop up their chests, and lift their noses in the air when they walk. This is when their vanity is still at a juvenile stage, when it is superficial, merely on the outside, which is quite different from the perfidious vanity within. You have people who are seemingly boastful, who display a childlike pretense of omnipotence, but who disintegrate before the Just. Not so the truly vain who may exhibit manners, humility, and gentility, but whose ego is calcified inside. In this case, the devil no longer holds them by the scruff of the neck to bring their noses up. It would be much too obvious that he is in control. In such cases, he asks vanity to manage with less oxygen. He deflates their lungs and lets them slump, to have them feign humility, while vanity thrives within.

Now you can more fully appreciate the meaning behind my unorthodox behavior discussed earlier. Grabbing the man by the coat was a means to humble him very quickly before the evil impulse could cause devastating damage. How did the man react to my mixing in his business? I had his impulse so intrigued; it stood there, watching me brutalizing the man. It figured that I was doing its job, which is exactly as I had planned. This is an old Jewish subterfuge.

The thing that mattered most was that I lifted the vain man over an imaginary fence, away from the sphere of influence of his impulse. I did it only to make him aware of the feasibility of the jump. Someone had to do it for him. His forceful, old fashioned, predictable ways were no match for the devil. A few more wrong turns and his knowledge would have become the devil's property.

The man was incomparably more knowledgeable than I, and there was a great chance that he would have resisted me. I had to take him to some other place where we would be equal, where he could hear me. There he would see me, not just as another debater crossing his path, but as I really am, a spiritual brother. He became totally oblivious of his social status. He relaxed his defenses. He understood that I had come to rescue him, and that I neither sought honor nor gain in doing so. It was an awesome sight to see such a distinguished person being tumbled over by the ant that I am. I felt shame. I was ready to apologize, but I withheld my sensibilities. I silenced my rational mind to do the job. I could not afford to ask myself if I would succeed or not. I positioned myself and I jumped.

Call it a leap of faith, or folly, whatever the nature of that moving force may be, what mattered most is that I set my mind to liberate what was kept prisoner, and quickly, before it acquired even more evil characteristics.

For in that instant, but in that instant only, the jump confers on one the title of *Tzaddik*, since the folly or the faith of the moment purifies one's intentions to a degree where body and soul, action and thought, become one and the same. The devil has no authority over such a union. This is the reason why, by virtue of such a fusion, the true *Tzaddikim* can leap over obstacles as though they were nonexistent.

The jump is not subject to failure, not when the soul itself takes the initiative. The language it produces neither cajoles nor rebukes. It is ancient, and it speaks a truth which heals. This is my recollection of the way we spoke in Morocco, one of the rare places where the world of the *Zohar* filled the air. This was the air on which we were weaned. This was the air that gave spirit to our speech. If our language was rich, it was because, aside from having been derived from our sacred literature, it combined the voice of one tightly knit people, dead and living, before it was emitted through one's mouth, as one's true voice, a voice that was sometimes distinct, potent, permissive, and unselfish. It was a relatively modest speech which made no scholarly quotes. Meanwhile, and I have been witness to this, it is in the house of the poor that the food is the tastiest. Nothing there is *de rigueur*. You can speak your mind; none of your remarks will turn offensive. What may look like an insult is, in reality, a communication of love in disguise.

It may be the sudden realization of life's benevolence to you, thus causing an excess of life that pours out of you, that has you express yourself so unreservedly. This is to alert the heart to receive its share of the feast. In context, outrageous language opens up closed chambers in the mind, where the true self is exiled, so that one remark, which has the tone of slander, can trigger the highest elevation.

Among the Jews of Morocco, it was not rare to change expressions of love into insults. We could not bring ourselves to use clichés; so we played at reversing the orders of meanings in our search for the words which would give justice to our sentiments. I recall how this extravagant form of speech was astutely used by my father when guests gave too many compliments about my mother's cooking; how he neutralized people's excess with an excess of his own. He would shift the mood by wondering why the soup was cold or lacked salt, to protect my mother to ward off envy or to elevate her to a realm higher than that of a mere cook. The mundane remarks of guests, as I recall, seemed to focus him on her true worth. This was his way of showing appreciation. He trusted that she would decipher the code. What is certain is that she was not starved for psychological uplift.

In any event, too many compliments are bad for the immune system. Beyond a certain point, praise weakens the reflexes that guard against the damaging insults from the outside world. An antidote to an insult is another insult, with love this time, to nullify it. To give a more concrete example, you tell the whole truth to a friend about himself—something no one would dare say to him, something that would normally hurt—before someone else throws it at him with evil intention. From your mouth, it is a preventive cure; from someone else, it is poison. The evil inclination waits for the opportune time to remind your friend of things he would rather forget. Anticipating such an attack, you drag it all out in the open and ridicule it. You make light of it. This is a new version of your friend's faults. This one, however, has a redeeming tone to it. And so, when the evil one comes along with *his* version, it's hopelessly old hat, *passé*, and therefore harmless.

The subterfuge works on oneself as well. It could happen, for instance, that while you are conversing with a group of people, you might suddenly come to grips with the enormity of one of your deficiencies and find yourself compelled to voice it in public. You choose to demystify it that way. However, the minute you open your mouth, someone, or perhaps everyone, might tell you how unfair you are to yourself, that you are actually doing fine. You want to explain your intentions, but that only serves to make it worse. You are frustrated over the fact that the people you are conversing with judge aberrant what is natural to you. You can tell that they are sincerely alarmed for you, as for themselves. The truth is that they are not willing to criticize you so readily in the midst of a casual talk. If that is the direction they will eventually have to take, they want to take it on *their* terms. Meanwhile, they spoiled your natural desire to trim yourself down to true size, thus denying you the privilege of journeying from your public persona to your true measure before God. The false situation that it creates deprives everyone present of a spiritual elevation. Everyone misses the opportunity to witness the birth of a new moment, a rare event, which can only take place in an ideal situation, in the midst of true companionship, when no one is on the defensive, when vanity is utterly absent. That is how truly "new" insights on the spiritual realm are born: when thought is no longer under the influence of the too physical "I." In seeing you make yourself so light on the world, heaven will contemplate the possibility to declare that something new has been born under the sun.

O n the occasion of the anniversary of the passing of
Rabbi Shimon Bar Yohai, the Lubavitcher Rebbe
spoke about the imminence of the last moments of exile. He
explained how the evil forces are now giving their fiercest
fight ever, right before the end, knowing that it is the
darkest time of night right before dawn. He cautioned us to
be as alert as those evil forces are as regards the imminence
of that final moment. On my way back home, I thought of
how the dark forces are such experts in having us believe
that our redemption is far off, how we have an impossibly
high mountain to climb, when in reality, it is just a hill. The
moment we take that hill, we win the battle. This is a
convention of war. No mountains, no country or city, just
that hill. And the news will spread wide that redemption has
begun.

Then I thought of how we all have in us the power
to leap over the frontiers that block our vision of the true
world. For my part, it began to store up in my youth from
different sources; certainly from my parents, with their
unrestricted love and self sacrifice. They were ready to die so
we could live. This transpired in their casual talk. "I die for
you; drink your soup," my mother would say, or, "Finish
your cereal; I'll be a sacrifice to you." When we were sick,
she would pray to be inflicted with the disease instead of us.
Hearing that, our fears took flight and we felt better. It was
partly thanks to that spirit of self sacrifice that we learned to
appreciate the excellence of light over darkness; that we saw
how fate could be altered with a single prayer. Add to that
the person of the Just, whose sole presence puts every force,
good or bad, in its proper perspective. All of this, and the
light of *Shabbat* and holy days, taught us as children to
discern the subtle manifestations of evil and their respective

antidotes. We watched evil shifting about, existing and non-existing, bluffing and sincere; moving between illusion and reality with the addition or subtraction of one deed, or of one single proton of hatred or love, because evil starves or subsists on such minute differences. Hence, it may be that the grand finale is being held back by one tiny component which has been willfully displaced, or by a single coin which has yet to be given with good intention by one certain person to one specific cause.

W HERE IT IS told how the main protagonist, a perfectly sane person, proceeds to awaken the entire population of a town through his uncanny behavior. He gets the job done by playing the idiot. His way to communicate his message consists mostly of transforming thought into apparently unrelated actions. At some point of the narrative, he transfigures himself into a dog, to redeem the townspeople. At another point, an incident happens that seems to belong in the domain of the legendary, but turns out to be quite real. The narrative ends with a purely imaginary episode about false gods who are blown away in midair in a three-ring circus to the delight of the spectators.

THE HIGH ROAD

OR MANY YEARS, my thoughts were often focused on the phenomenon of memory. The way I saw it, memory reigned sovereign in the metaphysical realm. It helped me to solve all of my existential probing. On occasion, I would meet people who shared my special interest in the subject, but they were not as driven as I. It appeared to me that their interest in memory was not essential and immediate. I long desired to meet someone who would truly be as obsessed by the subject, and eventually, he appeared.

He turned out to be completely absorbed by the subject of memory. He had traveled throughout the world to gather all of the material that he could find. Knowing of his interest, a mutual acquaintance advised him to pay me a visit. We chatted for an entire afternoon. He took some notes. He might have been preparing a thesis, or perhaps a book. I recall that he had close ties with a university. They could have hired him to scout the field. By the time we met, he had already gathered hundreds of pages of notes, most of which, as I later came to understand, were of a scientific nature. He himself had a very scientific mind, for each time the discussion took a metaphysical swerve, he wrinkled his forehead, and I would lose him, but not for long. The instant that he identified my interpretation of memory as being in some coincidental way similar to his own, he would almost pass out from pleasure.

It may have been one of the last times that I spoke with so much excitement and at such length about memory. I remember having inserted many stories and anecdotes between descriptions. I took the long way around, made connections, even digressions, which I thought were indispensable for a better understanding of the underlying function of memory. There was no way that I could speak more directly to the point. I had no means to do so. Besides, even if I could, in matters of acquiring or imparting authentic knowledge, the direct route is not always the shortest. At times, the longest way is the shortest way. In the interim, in the distance of time, the intellect gets the chance to be truly built up. The distance covered is commensurate with how much time it will take to build the vessel. Inside that vessel, the collective facts and visions are real. They work as points of reference and relay that make for a fluent and faithful reading of memory.

Unlike the Just, who are the true repository of memory, who speak in detours only because people's vessels are not apt to receive that intelligence all at once, I am a broken vessel, who must resort to circuitousness to find my own way around. My memory is that of an archaeologist by comparison. Each fragment that I unearth calls for the next, until I finally face the complete form. It is, I have to admit, a second rate approach for recovering lost intelligence. Nevertheless, it is a reliable one, insofar as it presents all the facts, all the pieces, in which case I am assured that the memory has been captured.

Most of what was said between my visitor and me has been, alas, lost, which gladdens me in some ironic way, in the sense that it compels me to start from scratch again, with new combinations which will hopefully offer an abode for things misplaced. There are many gates to Jerusalem, and there are many methods to cure the same disease, but enough preamble. Let us begin to gather the pieces.

Let's look at the Europe of two or three centuries ago, when the Jewish communities were devastated by poverty and by the constant fear of persecution. Worse still was the mood of distrust, the shattered hopes that had followed in the wake of a chain of false messiahs. It is easy to understand how, under such circumstances, morale could sink so low. The scholars, the elite who held the light of tradition, remained isolated from the common folk, and were therefore unable to convey to them the joy contained within those ancient teachings which they had been entrusted to preserve.

Then came the master, the holy Baal Shem Tov, to irrigate abandoned fields. He proceeded to transmit to common folk, in their own terms, what had been previously reserved for the select few. His rationale was clear: The same Father in Heaven, who gives clever people the capacity to understand, also creates the feeble mind and grants it no less right to share in the divine feast. Upon bringing to light the challenge, the Baal Shem Tov also unearthed the key: that special language by means of which the poor are allotted their spiritual portion, undefiled and unabridged.

The renaissance sparked by the Baal Shem Tov was fired by twin concerns. One, of course, was his love for his people. Had that been all, he might have thought it enough to spoon-feed the needy with the wealth of his own wisdom, but beyond that, he saw how heaven itself was suffering from excess holiness, or rather from our failure to raise up vessels into which the holy could descend. With small words attuned to small people, for the sake of heaven as well as man, he let the job be done. When the holy was finally allowed to penetrate to the depths where it belongs, its effect on the demeanor of those it touched was extraordinary. Housed in such modest surroundings, heaven was made a neighborhood. It became a daily occurrence for simple folk to ascend there on ladders of wood, or to arrive through open doors from adjacent rooms. No high powered lens was required to gaze into the infinite. Simple people were ideal chariots to transport the sacred, with never a self-thought, for they did not suffer from the vanity with which the gifted are apt to be plagued. They could travel in an instant through time to Sinai, and fall on their faces, trembling as if they had just received the Law. Just yesterday they were slaves to Pharaoh. Today they were free. The messiah was not a fable for these good people, or a possible dream of times to come; for them, redemption was now. Cunning minds might contend that they were merely naive. I would say, rather, that they bore the mark of wisdom: a good memory of the future, as well as of the past. To bind past events with those that must inevitably come, to fuse the two extremes of time and bring them to peace with the present, is to partake of the feast prepared by the Baal Shem Tov, the saintly teacher of the rich and the poor, who revealed that *memory is redemption*.

There is no limit to what memory can achieve. It is the source, the common font which, when tapped, can resolve all contradictions, and remind all people that they are at once equal and unique. Bound to our past, assured of our future, we are freed to become ourselves. One who remembers his origin in dust and ashes, and his end as a nest for worms, becomes humble enough to be crowned a king. Memory is the medium of a settled mind. It is the best medicine, too, for no matter who or what the agent of healing may be, real cure is affected by the strength that is found within. It is a process of reawakening to the model of health that is stored within our genes.

But how soon memory slips away, when we are hit with some passing misfortune. One might be snubbed inadvertently by a tactless friend, and in a moment of emotional upset lose sight of all the good that has accrued from a lifelong friendship. Or a son might forget all the care his parents gave him, after castigation or a clash. He bears the hurt in his heart, and survives by assuming a posture of indifference while, unknown to him, the hurt turns to hatred and rage. Years pass, and he roams, rootless and estranged. Even in the midst of his successes, he is susceptible to depression and disease. Trauma taints his vision, and he cannot see the whole. He will find correctives that achieve half the cure, will move from contrivance to contrivance, all futile, unless he turns a blind eye to his grievances, so truly as to forget all insults, and takes the high road. That, if I may be so bold, is the prerequisite phase of memory at its best: to forget the bad and remember the good.

But let us get back, for a moment, to the impoverished age of European exile. The general populace in those days had become somewhat disengaged from the web of memory, and therefore tended to fall back upon the prevailing winds of the time. Imagination was on fire. There were demons dwelling in the attics, and devils stalking the streets. Distraught mothers of skittish young girls would swear that their daughters were possessed. While *dybbuks* played hide and seek, people would slit open their mattresses for the cash to shop for amulets, or to pay the exorcist his fee. Audiences, avid and ingenuous, would stand spellbound as storytellers spun wild fantasies before their eyes.

Imagination was the opiate, and it served its purpose well. It gave rest and regeneration to the depressed. It was a snuff to the strait-laced. It was all that, and more, for those who could reap neither nourishment nor incentive from their tradition. It was often used as an escape. Therefore it had its limitations. In those days, it meandered like a ship on a leisure cruise. At its best, it looked like an archer shooting arrows in all directions, hoping to spear some secret information. Thinking he has hit the target, he runs to the spot where he believes the prey has fallen and meets with a mirage. He repeats his attempt over and over again and yet never seems to be disappointed, because for him, the capture is not as important as the excitement his experience provides.

By comparison, today's imagination seems less obsessive. It derives little from superstition or religion, as it did then. Yesterday's dreamer is an extinct breed. The few who are left attribute the too rapid loss of creative imagination to science. They accuse science of being single-minded. They can't stand the fact that, nitty gritty, it has appropriated for itself all five dimensions. They cannot forgive it for subordinating the human vision to the unremitting scientific suggestions of the machine.

As imagination and science debate, memory, which is the mother of them both, stands aside, to observe their performance and growth. She towers above their path. From her vantage point, the mind is galvanized by what it sees. There, it is easier to view how history could, at any moment, reach a full term; how redemption is only a matter of midwifery. There we are given to observe souls slipping off their corporeal cloaks and leaping suddenly to their primordial origin, to then bounce back and don plain clothes again, thrusting blithely past the present toward the future. Once there, they proclaim the climax of their life on earth. Moments later they swing back to the Source, where they arrive as diaphanous as the wind. On each trip, in their human form, they carry with them further news of realities yet to be revealed. They travel through the present moment at such a speed that they must resort to metaphor in order to give weight to the messages they bear.

A metaphor is a transfer that can only be carried out by flesh and blood. We humans ship truth, properly transformed, to distant places. In heaven there is no darkness, and therefore no need to use oblique figures of speech. Angels are not charged with the perilous mission of smuggling the holy from a place of bliss to a place of crime, but we spend quick instants in darkness, quick instants in light. We have not yet begun to arrive and then we are already gone. We swing like pendulums whose speed is determined by the urgency of our mission. We stutter, in apprehension of not being able to fully express what it is we mean to say. The clarity of our visions and dreams depends upon the skill with which we maintain balance between two extremes. Our swaying is sometimes steady, at other times erratic, according to our degree of conscientiousness, and the depth from which our memory is revealed.

But memory is not something that is exclusively reserved for the mind. The body also has ways to store it. It can either run in the blood, the genes, the kidneys, or the liver. It resides in the hands of the weaver and the pianist. It is a prime mover in the hand of the giver of charity. Old age cannot dissuade the foot from carrying out its mission. Now that every deed has purified the body in corresponding measure, memory turns to redemption.

The process of remembrance begins from the place that we choose, providing that its actions are carried out with pleasantness, for memory is lost in anger. Pleasantness, however, does not need to obliterate one's strength or character or revolutionary zeal. At the core, we Jews are revolutionaries. We stand up to rebel against injustice and stagnation of thought. Our insurrectionary character has never let us fall into complacent forgetfulness. It is with that spirit that the outnumbered Maccabees defeated a mighty army. It is also with that spirit that we cannot tolerate the seemingly wise passivity and placidity of the compromiser. It is evident that, in such a case, you have to resist the temptation to seek justice. At times, however, you must act, especially when memory itself is at stake. You must not spare the reproof. You must revolt to remember. You can show kindness without falling into easy acceptance of people's cowardice. Accept them as they are, but at the same time prepare your rebellion. Do not fight the person. Confront the forgetfulness that is within them. Fight the Amalek in them and obliterate *his* memory. He is one evil force which seeks to erase any good feeling the nations might have for the Jews. He attacked us when we came out of Egypt. Now he is in the air, making suggestions, telling people of our vulnerability. He causes rifts among us. The worst he does is to deaden the heart, to the point of training it to hate for no reason at all. As opposed to common hatred, which could just be an aspect of love that took ill, Amalek's instilled hatred has no roots. It comes from nowhere. All we know is that if it is aggravated by an ever-growing hole in the memory, there is only one antidote: you have to bang your head against the wall of your heart until your heart bleeds.

To illustrate, I recall having experienced a strong reaction to an otherwise insignificant event that put my life in total disarray. I had no one to blame for that incident but myself. It began with a phone call from a casual acquaintance who was making a routine inquiry about an upcoming lecture by a rabbi whom he championed. I went to that lecture. The rabbi was speaking in a feeble voice to a small group of regulars in his weekly evening class. He was a man of fragile constitution whose pale, emaciated face showed him to be a natural thinker, the kind of man who would readily win the trust of perplexed youth. While some took notes, and others fiddled with cassette recorders, the rabbi was visibly straining to make himself heard. After brief remarks, he threw open the discussion for questions. Apparently unaware of his frail condition and the difficulty he had in speaking, most of those present insisted on draining him of his energy with pseudo intellectual comments. There was one young man in particular who was doing most of the talking. Slouching in his chair, he prefaced his questions with long-winded, barely relevant explications of his point of view. In a confident, too casual tone of voice, with two fingers to his furrowed brow, he would formulate clever queries that were utterly out of keeping with his slovenly posture. His unpleasant demeanor, I decided, was a direct result of the lack of rapport between his body and his mind. His legs were spread wide and lifeless in front of him, as though out of control.

I felt that the talk was not accomplishing much. The rabbi obviously sensed the split in the young man, but did not seem to have the second wind to give impact to his thoughts. This audience seemed not to need intellectual stimulation but rather physical revivification. People's faces began appearing to me like disembodied talking heads. I grew restless and turned in my seat. I wanted to leave, but stayed out of respect for the rabbi. I withdrew into myself and began playing with my own thoughts. When occasionally I would awaken to check on what was being said, each time I saw the poor man being progressively swallowed by his audience. He was reduced from the commanding role of teacher to the impersonal impotence of a biofeedback machine.

Of the twenty or thirty young people who were there that night, most appeared to have been involved either in cults or other strange religions. They were cautious, skeptical, and in retrospect, it seems logical that they should have sought the kind of teacher who would make no strenuous demands. If they could not actually manipulate him, at least he was no threat. His innocuous nature simply accommodated their phobias and shortcomings. One thing is certain: he did not dilute the true significance of the Law, or shift personalities in the pulpit to harmonize with the times. In fact, he was very much himself, but like other public servants who fear to offend, he was afflicted with the habit of making suggestions in situations that call for commands. His gentle speech settled over their hypersensitive minds like strands of silk. He understood and accepted their limitations, but one can perhaps be too gracious, too timid. The loss of purpose outweighs the gain in trust. With bolder language and more acerbic words, he may not have been able to create such a climate of ease and equanimity, but he might have succeeded in jarring their memories. These young people, though loathe to admit it, had had their fill of pats on the back. They indulged in his dispensations like deprived children who crave attention after giving up on love. As I saw it, the rabbi had excelled in quenching their thirst for knowledge, but had failed to infuse their future actions with that selfless and quintessentially Jewish trait: a sense of urgency.

The lecture ended at the very moment that my head had begun to nod in sudden sleep. As I rose to leave and walked toward the exit, I heard a familiar voice coming from behind me. It was the young man with the sprawling feet, speaking to two others of his own age. "I've never met anyone who can move me the way he does," he said.

A female voice to my left replied, "Thank God we have him."

"He knows me better than I know myself," the man said. "I wish more people could come and hear him."

"There aren't many men like that left in the world," said another voice to my right.

Other such accolades accompanied me all the way down the stairs and out of the building. Their tributes were perfectly timed to convince me beyond a doubt that I had judged the rabbi too quickly. I had unfairly evaluated a man who obviously knew what he was doing, and who did it quite well. Every one of their comments added to my guilt.

"I feel like dancing," someone said. Other voices chimed in, "Yes, let's dance!" I took a deep breath of fresh air and slipped away.

My car was parked half a block away. As I placed the key in the door, I turned my head and saw a half dozen men twirling in a circle in the dark of night. The wind blew unevenly in my direction, carrying with it a Hasidic melody sung slightly out of tune. Tiny drops of rain had begun to cover the windshield. Without turning on the wipers, scolding myself for my unjust criticism and chronic impatience, I drove away.

I spent most of the next day downcast. I had slighted a good and honest man. It caused me to profoundly doubt the value of all my writing and public speaking, and I wondered how I would ever face audiences again. The guilt was bludgeoning me. Moments of irresolution and uncertainty had, at times, disabled me, but never to such an extent.

In the months following that rabbi's class, I spent much time running errands, and paid more attention to my family and to making a living. Soon I began to enjoy my new lifestyle, and to forget the ordeal that had led me to do it. In the process, I also found some time to reflect, as objectively as possible, upon my future plans. Eventually I recovered by reconnecting with an old dream, an ambition of my youth that has never really left me. Then it was vague. It was like the hoarse, insistent pounding of the sea that exhorts young dreamers to set sail, and as mysterious as an unknown song begging to be aired. For more than three decades, beginning in my adolescence, I had made attempts to write that song, but never thought myself ready. At a certain point, I decided that it would take me until old age before I would be prepared to do it justice. The paralysis that set in after that night at the lecture was just the final hammer blow.

I might have kept my resolve to let go of the dream, had it not been for the rapid deterioration of memory that I perceived in the people around me. It is true that I am uneven. I am half raw and half burnt. I had to come out. While writing these lines, the question I still ask myself is whether people will share my concern enough to read between the missing notes. Can a crudely fashioned man such as myself succeed in singing the song?

The ancient sages look down on me from their heavenly portals. They are amused, but perturbed at my insolence. One of them says, "Who gave that clown permission to speak?"

"Sounds like a barking dog," says another, "but look how his audience attends to his howls."

A third sage, though engrossed in an enormous book, has overheard the conversation. He lifts his head for a moment and peers down at me. "Is there such a shortage of teachers that we're forced to put up with this?"

All three stare in silence for a moment before returning to their holy books. "We all agree," says the first, "that he is an empty headed fool, but consider the generation in which he lives ... and read what it says here."

He thrusts a thick volume across the table and quotes, "In a place where there are no men, strive to be a man."

It is the eldest of the three who decrees, "Then let our friend walk his road, and arrive where his feet will take him. Chances are it will never make a man of him, but let him yelp, as long as it helps our cause."

At another time I would have been willing to undergo a more protracted penance, and accept the sense of unworthiness. I might have even gone so far as to change occupations, but not then. I had paid dearly, sacrificing almost a year, following my unspoken polemic against the soft-spoken rabbi. If I were to decide to first outgrow all my deficiencies before facing audiences again, I would have had to wait a lifetime. I had no choice but to go ahead with my original intent to speak with a spirit of revolt in my heart. I figured that at that stage my immaturity would prove more productive toward that end than whatever good qualities I might have claimed.

With my quandary half resolved, partially wise and partially absolved, I might now venture to symbolize the archetypal incarnation of the Jew in the grip of exile, to dramatize for all people a brief, unsweetened version of our biblical narrative. I will stand between the poles of light and darkness, and there secure intelligence with which to trap evil at dawn and at dusk. Perchance truth will then be recognized by the naked eye and divinity by the flesh. Perhaps I will live as a Jew must live, and narrate my life with pure action, and my blood will overwhelm my irresolution, animate my thoughts, and rouse my mouth to speak the long forgotten language of the soul. I articulate with words, or with dance, to include everyone: the skeptic, the perplexed, and the scholar as well.

For that I dress in black and white, attire myself in light and darkness, to resemble a letter of the *Aleph Bet*.

One by one I dance out all the letters, then reverse their sequence, and follow that with a verse. For a melancholy bystander, I write page after page of holy texts with my feet, not stopping until blood reddens his cheeks. He takes a liking to reading my dance, and asks for more than I can afford to give, but when I try to signal that I have to pause, he is too absorbed to notice. I fear that I cannot satisfy him, for my breath is short and my legs fatigued. I begin to slow the pace. Suddenly he takes charge of the dance. Now I am his puppet. He maneuvers me like a bouncing ball. I am about to collapse from exhaustion, yet here I am building up speed, trapped by my own will to please.

He has me dance in moments all that I have learned in a lifetime. I dance out thoughts and emotions, combine water with fire, and tie together heaven and earth. He comes near me, clapping hands and jerking to the beat of my unconventional interpretation of a scriptural verse. His lack of rhythm throws me so off balance that I have to constantly change my pace to cover for his awkwardness. A sudden surge of joy brims over his pathetic countenance, revealing a hint of dementia. I grasp his hands, and together we compose holy patterns that swallow his affliction, until he begins to look like himself again. It will take another hour, at least, to succeed in suffusing him with enough happiness to last him for one exile. But my lungs are burning and my knees are weak. He senses my weariness, pulls my head to rest against his shoulder, and we twirl, so fast that we form one body. I am only mind. My feet no longer touch the ground, and the music grows louder as we play that old Jewish game of being caught and freed at the same time.

The world has yet to discover a more powerful expression of freedom than Jewish dance. It is a dance that frees both the dancer and the onlooker. It is also a powerful cure. The sense of emergency lends it a very special character. Such a dance was not called for in the past, when it was considered a significant achievement to have a positive influence on one person in a crowd of a hundred. Now that life within seems to be disintegrating, saving *one* life is tantamount to denying it to the other ninety nine. Now we have to rouse the multitudes to dance. We must open up to a new configuration of intellect. We must ignite fires in dead hearts with dancing thoughts. Jewish dance is known for its power to unite even enemies.

In the meantime, intelligence won't be wasted. On the contrary, it will only gain by going out into the streets. It will wear street clothes. It will come dressed as a harlequin to prepare the people for the coming festivity. The colors of its costume will entertain the wrecked senses of the perplexed. It will amuse them with bright flags before flipping them over to reveal the basic black and white of unequivocal truth.

In my eagerness to reduce intelligence to its simplest possible expression, I had recurring daydreams about a man, an alter ego, but he was bolder, older and wiser than me. I made him my ideal, for he had managed to constrict his intellectual faculties to such an extent that he was mistaken for an idiot. I would have such a man live through all sorts of adventures. Some of those adventures were purely imagined. Some, however, were souped up versions of my own experiences.

In one of those dream adventures, he appears in the central square of a small town, in the middle of the night. He whistles loudly. Everyone is awakened. Then, with a second whistle, he shatters plaster moldings and chandeliers, bringing mirrors and paintings crashing to the floor.

Landlords and tenants pour into the square. They run toward the sound of the whistling and find the idiot standing by the fountain. They form a circle around him. Someone runs to call the police.

"He's the one!" says an elderly man in robe and slippers.

An old woman in a dressing gown steps forward, clutching a silver box filled with jewels. "Why," she asks the idiot, "are you destroying our property?"

"Yes," says a policeman who has just arrived, "why indeed?" He looks around in bewilderment, his hands resting on his hips.

The crowd grows dense and restless. A man in his late thirties pushes through and grabs the idiot fiercely by the collar, screaming, "You have destroyed ten years of work with your stupidity!" He shakes a crumpled sheaf of papers in front of the idiot's face. "This is all that is left of a manuscript which was to teach the world!"

Just when they are about to lynch him, the idiot surprises them all by speaking with the gentlest of voices: "I beg you, pardon me," he says. "To destroy your property was the furthest thing from my mind. The only reason I came to town was because I had run out of food, and I would have left as silently as I arrived, had I not seen dark hosts gathering in the sky, preparing your annihilation. The damage has been great, I can see, but it would have been far worse if I had not frightened them away with my whistle."

A distinguished man with an air of authority and a well-trimmed graying beard plants himself firmly in front of the idiot. He lifts his hand to command attention. "If I understand his words correctly," he says to the assembled, "this imbecile claims to have been sent to save us." And to the idiot, "Answer me this, then: If you are really the rescuer that you portray yourself to be, where does that power come from anyway? From a holy place or from somewhere else?"

The idiot's face lights up, as though he is deeply pleased to have provoked such a query. "Rest assured," he says with a smile, "that I claim no power of my own. What has happened here is not done by my own will or calculation. I do only as I am told. I will gladly clarify my actions for all of you, if you care to listen."

"In my heyday," he went on, "I had *everything*: wealth, glory and wisdom. I could read minds and predict events. Thousands took my word as law. I was a mystic. I could leap from mountain to mountain until the day, by Divine Providence, I met a sage, in whose presence I lost all my powers. I had come to see him out of curiosity, to get a blessing from him and then depart. I was on my way to Jerusalem to realize an old dream, to learn Kabbalah with the true Kabbalists, but the sage advised me not to leave the country. I was trapped. There was no way that I could go against the word of a *Tzaddik*. He advised me to learn for only an hour or two a day. The rest of the time, I should devote to other people. When I argued that an hour was too little for me, he said, "Scholars we have. We need good horses!" He spoke of how redemption was at hand, and I had an important role to play.

"You can't imagine the joy his words brought to me. If my inclination and my dream had been to reach the highest possible form of intelligence, in his presence it became a certainty that I would never see that day. Not in this incarnation and not in the next. What a relief that was! He cleared my head. I went out of there as a free man. I danced in the streets. I howled. I sang old opera arias, and I whistled. I whistled so much that my mind became an empty chamber. Within that emptiness, which was devoid of all my intellectual acrobatics, I suddenly made an extraordinary and sublime contact with the sage, my Rebbe. For just an instant, I ceased to be a separate self." Saying that, the idiot pauses and lowers his eyes. For a moment he is silent, deep in thought. He turns to rinse his face in the refreshing waters of the fountain, and then speaks to the crowd again. "I must take my leave," he announces, now choked with emotion. "Hasten, please, to make way for me, for I have two more assignments today."

The people stand aside to let the idiot pass. He walks a few steps and suddenly stops. Tears are streaming down his cheeks. "The war is raging!" he cries. "And you are still debating with me! Don't fight me! Fight the enemy, but know how to do it, for he is ... illusion. This is the reason why he appears so overwhelming. So take my advice. Have no pity. Use your breath. Whistle as I do. With the breath of pleasure we have sinned, and through breath we shall be redeemed!"

With that, the idiot whirls around and peers through the crowd, scanning the faces as though expecting to find someone. A woman lowers her shoulder, to reveal behind her the receding hairline of the writer whose manuscript was lost. The idiot points a trembling finger in his direction, and the woman moves sheepishly to the side. The writer's face, now in full view, turns green.

"And you," the idiot says, "be sure to despise evil with every fiber of your being. You'll see that it will make you a better writer. As you run from evil, you will acquire rhythm, through which your soul will speak more freely. You will know great fame, yet remain humble, because as you wholeheartedly thrust yourself away from evildoing, your best traits will gain momentum. For you, any other path is a minefield, where vanity explodes with every step you take. Thus unburdened, you will enjoy yourself immensely. You will travel on clouds, if you should so choose!"

There is a rustling amongst the crowd. An old woman, a librarian, fights her way through the mass of people and stands in front of the idiot. She cocks her head back and to the side, folds one arm across her waist, and brings the other hand to her chin. "Forgive the intrusion," she says with self importance, "but it behooves me to say a word or two, before this takes a turn for the worse." She gestures in the direction of the writer. "I have groomed this gentleman from his youth, and I have seen him blossom into the finest writer of his time. Now you come, carrying on with grandiloquence about clouds and evil forces, to lure the very spirit of genius from our midst!"

The idiot stares unflinchingly into her eyes, with the faintest trace of a smile. She returns his gaze.

"Has it never occurred to you," she says, "that what is right for one person may be wrong for another? Is that so hard to understand, even for an idiot? You want to be a clown? Fine! I don't doubt that your act will win you millions of admirers, myself among them. But why must you interfere with this man's art? Please, a hundred times please, do not destroy his gift. Let him finish his masterpiece!"

The writer is not given time to savor the flattery, for the idiot's eyes are on him. Aborted pride turns quickly to embarrassment. All at once, he is inundated by the bizarre sensation that he has already met with this man. But where? Was it in his dreams? No, it was in this life. Where then? All the while, an incoherent stream of words has been coming out of the old lady's mouth. The idiot walks away and the writer follows him. They disappear from the place. The townspeople return to their homes.

The writer has had a difficult time since his encounter with the idiot. He has not lifted his pen in years. He even finds it hard to write a letter to his family. Wondrous thoughts arise, some powerful enough to awaken the dead, but rather than write them down, he dismisses them, bringing them as burnt offerings. No residue of those thoughts remains to inspire his former readers, who now mourn his departure from the literary scene. Word has gone out that he has been kidnapped by a secret sect. There has also been a rumor circulating that he has been begging for charity on the streets of Jerusalem. From time to time, he is tempted to offer people some peace of mind by tossing them some factual news, but he restrains himself because, you see, on that fateful day, as the idiot looked at him with his piercing eyes, he completely lost contact with his work, or rather, it all became meaningless to him.

The most amazing thing he had yet to discover was that the persona of the idiot happened to mysteriously cohere with an undefined, yet consistent, recurring thought that had accompanied him in his youth.

This was precisely the same pounding thought that had him start to write in the first place, but he had lost it. Nothing he put on paper ever satisfied him. The more recognition he received, the more difficult it became for him to give some sense to his writings, and then, in the presence of the idiot, the sensation had returned. A few days went by before he could finally figure out that he knew the idiot from deep inside himself, not in the sense that they were one and the same person, but that he had become the idiot's relay.

Soon after their original encounter, a metamorphosis began to take place. He found it hard to express his thoughts. Whenever he attempted to put his thinking process in gear, the rush of ruminations would reach his mouth much too quickly, thus causing him to utter sheer nonsense. His infirmity forced him to search for other modes of communication. He learned the usefulness of action and practiced it in ways seldom seen before. By restricting the use of the intellect, he conferred a new dimension on the deed. Needless to say, his wisdom grew at a remarkable pace. Even more remarkable is the fact that no one noticed that it did. Little did his entourage know how much effort it would take him to resist his old habit of thinking beyond the measure of his deeds.

Because he had abstained from expressing himself with the written word for so long, the little bits of Scripture he learned ignited his intellect like a bellows firing up a furnace. Sometimes in his studies he would practically fall into a trance, to the point of letting go of his soul. On such occasions he would offset the undesired effect by standing on his head. He would feel rather silly doing it, but it was the only way he knew to keep his soul from taking off. Ever since this began to happen, he would only study alone, from fear he would have to perform public headstands when his head threatened to explode.

For many years he traveled from town to town, country to country, to speak in people's houses, in synagogues, even in theaters. Once he crossed paths with a star rabbi, a story teller, a *maggid*, famed throughout the world for his quick wit. It happened in the most prestigious synagogue of a capital city. The maggid stood up on that memorable Saturday morning and began with a few jokes which had the audience roaring with laughter. He followed that with a long and rather tragic story that had comical overtones. All this was later woven into a novel personal interpretation of a verse from the Torah portion of the week. He was so involved in his subject that the blood vessels of his face and neck bulged to the point of nearly bursting out. The audience was delighted. Everyone stood up and began to applaud. It was like theater. Nothing like this had ever happened on a Shabbat in that synagogue. Little did the people of the congregation know what was awaiting them. The moment they sat down again, the maggid closed his eyes, took a deep breath, and began to deliver what must have been the most frightening harangue ever heard in Jewish history.

He gave such a lurid description of hell that he had everyone literally suffocating and sweating. Three ladies who sat in the front row fainted when he described how high the temperature was. Then he told one long story about a young sinner who refused to repent even after half of his family and one of his best friends had died accidentally, all because of his actions. The sinner finally repented after the rabbi made him realize that all of those deaths were retribution for his sins. He had the entire congregation in the palm of his hand. By then, all faces had turned white from extreme fear. A bad smell began to ooze out from an unknown source, but only the writer noticed it.

When the writer's turn to speak arrived, he could not be found. They finally caught him reaching for the exit door and dragged him to the pulpit, where he stood shaking, not knowing what to say. He had been trying to recuperate from the maggid's overpowering speech when they urged him to begin. He opened his mouth but nothing would come out. If he could only think. His confusion should have been apparent. A few moments more and who knows what would have happened to him? He was about to black out from humiliation and timidity when, all of a sudden, he remembered what his teacher, the idiot, had once told him: "Run from evil and do good." He screamed loud, deep within himself, to break the walls of darkness which were entrapping him. He heard the din of galloping horses in his head. Soon, an avalanche of words began to roll out of his mouth.

Every word was blasted out by a powerful combustion that was fueled by an utter abhorrence of evil. He went on speaking until the damage that the manic *maggid* had inflicted upon the congregants' souls was completely undone.

The damage had been quite serious indeed because the maggid was not a *Tzaddik*. His fear of God was not total, certainly not enough to enable him to give such a rebuke. As opposed to the *Tzaddik*, who draws his fear from Eden, the same fear that Adam experienced when facing God, the maggid's fear was the result of a combustion generated by his own inherent phobias and undigested food. With that low grade type of fear, he had managed to petrify those poor Jews, and bring them down to such an animal condition that their bodies emitted an unpleasant smell. The air had become so unbreathable that even the mixture of scents given off by the women's expensive perfumes and the men's fragrant colognes could not suppress the odor. But now the danger had passed. The writer stopped speaking only after he had verified that every face had gained its normal pinkish complexion. He ended his speech with a lengthy blessing for health, wealth and wisdom. He shook a few extended hands and then left the synagogue.

An old man is walking on a deserted road. His worn-out clothes are evidence that he is a beggar. The rooftops of the town toward which he is heading appear on the horizon. From a pocket, he removes an immaculate handkerchief and covers his mouth. As he walks steadfastly toward the town, his shoulders hunched, his face buried in the handkerchief, he is periodically seized with violent fits of coughing.

The beggar is none other than the legendary whistler, whose age and waning strength now prevent the practice of his former craft. Instead, he has totally given himself over to the task of collecting funds for the needy. It's a vexing occupation, but the old man does not complain. He actually views his present appointment as an unmitigated blessing. In begging for charity, he knows he paves the giver's road, bestowing life upon him, both in the here and the hereafter. He saves the miser from certain death, and forces diehard thinkers to face the deed.

Another coughing spell forces the beggar to stop by the side of the road to catch his breath. Standing still, with both hands in front of his face, he waits for the spasms to abate, then continues walking until he arrives at the town's gate. Slowly, he removes the handkerchief from his mouth, and takes small sips of air as he proceeds.

Inside the gate he is greeted by the explosive sounds of a fairground. Calliope music blasts from loudspeakers mounted over the entranceways to rides and games. There is skeetball, a batting cage, a rifle range, and a roller coaster, whose clacking wheels can barely be heard above the squeals of the passengers. There is the octopus, the parachute jump, the rocket ship, and the whirly gig, and the muffled rumble of all these metallic monsters vibrates inside the beggar's skull. There are more people present than the fairgrounds can contain. They push and shove and squeeze and squirm, trying in vain to form orderly lines for the rides. Everyone is eager to get a seat, the old folks even more than the young. They mount papier-mâché horses on merry-go-rounds, slapping painted wooden flanks with open palms, giggling.

At the far end of the field, the crowd makes way for two men. One is tall, bald, and clean shaven, and the other is short, with a trimmed beard and a roundish hat. The beggar recognizes immediately that these two are the mayor and the rabbi of the town. They walk side by side, visiting every booth and ride, pleased by what they see. The mayor is holding an ice cream sugar cone and the rabbi has a large pink puff of cotton candy. They smile and nod, wide-eyed, returning peoples' greetings, licking and biting, respectively, the former dabbing at the corners of his lips with a crumpled yellow napkin, the latter deftly plucking strands of spun sugar from his beard.

The beggar wends his way among the throng. A Talmudist is tossing baseballs at kewpie dolls. The Chief of Police, bare-chested, muscles bulging, is bench pressing barbells before dazzled young yeshiva boys. The rabbi's wife, holding a plucked chicken high in the air, breathes fire, and in a single blast, roasts the bird whole. Every face glows red, from rich and spicy foods, and from excessive laughter. Happiness sizzles in the early evening air like streaks of summer lightning, but the beggar feels uneasy. He lifts his eyes skyward, in prayer.

"Father in Heaven," he whispers, "grant success to my mission. Give me the necessary strength and patience to collect charity from every one of these people. Today they are joyful, and willing to give, but tomorrow they will avoid me as if I were the devil himself. They'll send their wives to the door and tell them to say: 'I'm sorry, my husband is resting. Could you please come back tomorrow, or in a week?', knowing I am weary and will probably not return. Therefore, gracious Father, place kindness in their hearts, that they may give with an open hand, and thereby be redeemed."

By nightfall, the beggar has amassed a heavy sack of coins. Standing by the gate as the fairground empties, he accepts a generous offer of bed and board, and is so tired from his long day's work that he falls asleep in the middle of his nightly prayer. He dreams that he is visited by an old beggar like himself.

"In my time," the other beggar begins to tell him in the dream, "these people never acted so badly toward one another. No one in this town ever went to bed hungry, or lacked for a place to sleep. There was a large house built especially for wayfarers, where anyone could stay as long as he wished. The townspeople used to sit and learn Scripture every day until noon, and then go to make their living. There was standing room only in the house of study. Even some Gentiles stood by the doors, intoxicated by the music of our learning. It was an exhilarating time, but it came to an end shortly after I fell ill and could no longer make the rounds. People began to backslide. The wealthy shut their ears to the cries of the needy. A man would hesitate to greet his neighbor for fear of actually helping him to have a pleasant day. The scholars became as vain and possessive as the rich, and even the poor grew proud. Seriousness became such a plague that dozens died from it every year. First, they would burn with a strange fever which produced no sweat, then their bones would dry up, turning brittle and black as charcoal. The calamity grew to such alarming proportions that the town council met in special session, trying to find a remedy. After days of deliberation, they decided that happiness was the answer, and that a grand amusement park would provide the cure. They called in the best engineers and construction crews, who erected the fair in one day. It was an instant success and the plague was checked in a few weeks.

"But a greater calamity was yet to come, and it caught me unawares. One morning I went to the forest, for meditation and peace. Once there, I began to notice, for the first time, an abominably overpowering stench issuing from the village. You might liken this phenomenon to that of burning food; people in the next room can be gasping from the smoke, while the cook stands by the stove and smells nothing.

"I died in that forest. It was a horrible death, by asphyxiation. You are strong, and not as old as I was then. To be safe, however, do not make the same mistake as I did. Never leave town for fresh air. It may prove fatal.

"One last bit of information before I depart," continued the elder beggar. "You surely noticed how artificial the joy of these people was. It is so beyond reality that it is pathetic. With their silly behavior, they hope to demonstrate that they are in the swim, that they can outdo us. Our bursts of joy, as you know, are upsurges of remembrance. I don't have to tell you that their false joy is the result of a deficient memory. They might have some memory left in their heads, but none of it has gone to their hearts. Nor, for that matter, to the rest of their body. Their head is selfish. The body has been left totally in the dark. They only have the head as storage room. Your mission, therefore, my dear colleague, consists of breaking these people with true laughter, until they regain their true identity. You must succeed, for this town happens to be a strategic place. You break them with joy and you will affect the entire planet."

At the first glimmer of dawn, the beggar awakes from his dream, dresses and hurries out to pray with the first quorum of early risers. He collects charity even as he prays, and afterwards stays his heart with cake and tea before slipping away to beg in other synagogues. Before long he begins to meet with his first difficulties. In one instance, a short-tempered sexton grabs his moneybag and flings it onto the street. In another, a congregant screams at him for interfering with the service, inciting others to howl as frantically as he. In most places he is instructed to wait until everyone has finished praying. But he is not intimidated. He knows too well the way people rush off to work, walking quickly past solicitors with listless, unseeing eyes, or tapping their pockets with a shrug that says, "nothing here". The beggar refuses to retreat before an initially unpleasant demeanor. He can tell who feigns fervor in prayer in order to avoid him. He plants himself in front of them, sometimes going so far as to mimic their artificial winces and furrowed foreheads. Vexed, each one finally throws a coin into his sack.

The work becomes more difficult later in the day, out on the streets, where reluctant passersby are not subject to the same pangs of guilt as those in confined areas. We find the beggar on the sidewalk, rattling his handful of coins in the midst of the morning rush. He literally leaps toward those who attempt to escape him, blocking their passage and stretching out his hand. With each one, he repeats the same gesture: he bends slightly toward the person, as though trying to catch his scent, then steps back to a more normal stance, and remains there, looking him straight in the eye until he makes his contribution. What he is in fact doing is smelling all the people he meets, sampling the odors on their clothes, to assess their worth.

It is said that the Messiah will have the ability to judge people not by what he sees or hears, but by the sense of smell. It is an infallible method that leaves no room for excuses or pleas of innocence. The beggar works in somewhat the same way,   except that his skill was acquired through his deficiencies, rather than by his righteousness.

Although he is old, there lingers within him a memory of the transgressions of his youth. There are still moments when fetid odors arise out of his past. Against these, he measures other people's sins by nuances of smell. The Messiah, however, like his saintly predecessors whose lives are similarly untainted by sin, will be spared the noxious smell of others' indiscretions. Since he will lack firsthand experience, Heaven will have to grant him the power to judge at least the spirit, if not the substance, sin. He will be like the wine-master who inhales only the sweet fragrance of a fine, finished wine yet with that remembers in detail every unpleasant stage of fermentation.

Though unsophisticated by comparison, the beggar's yardstick helps him to monitor the degree of immediacy of a person's problems, and to establish the precise number of coins he must give to be redeemed. It is astonishing how a mere monetary transaction can acquaint the contributor with the reality of redemption. Moments before, the contributor was ambling along, unmindful of his future, lunging here and there, seeking pleasure, lost in vague unfocused thought. Now suddenly, the abstract images that muddied his mind have vanished. The carnal eruptions have ceased. The abrupt dissolution of his dream state casts him down so low that for a moment he loses touch with his own identity, and with all existence. Having given of his money, he has died a little bit, and he therefore tricks death, which can only vanquish that which is defiantly alive. From this new vantage point, he can see more clearly. With a single coin, he has staked his claim on the imminence of redemption, and has discovered within himself the will to believe in the promised days.

A week has gone by, and the beggar has met with great success. There was not one passerby who did not give. Each working day, two moneybags were filled to the brim, one by midday and the second by dusk. He has been working ceaselessly, even into the night, never allowing himself to feel his fatigue, going from door to door until every town dweller has donated his share. All, that is, but one, a very wealthy Jew who is well known for not having dropped a copper in a charity box in quite a long time. He lives on a huge estate surrounded by high walls, some distance from town, and sees no one, save occasional visitors from foreign lands, most of them Gentiles, all of them as wealthy as himself.

T he beggar decides to visit the miser. He does not want to tell anyone of his intentions, but how would he go about it? He neither knows the way to the estate nor does he have the means to reach it. He is left with no alternative but to hire a coach. A time is arranged. The coachman, as one would expect, does not waste a moment to tell his wife, who tells her neighbors, who then tell the entire town.

It is a very hot afternoon. The beggar is standing in front of the miser's gate. He has no doubt that if he were to ring the bell, the servant would not only refuse him entrance, but would send the hounds after him. So he scales the high portal, and leaps, landing on his feet on the other side. From behind a row of pine trees, he hears the sound of splashing water. He weaves his way through coarse trunks and branches to find himself standing at the deep end of an enormous inlaid marble pool. A middle-aged man, tanned, with greying sideburns, steps out at the far end and executes gymnastic figures on the manicured turf, as he progresses in the direction of a large marble gazebo built in the style of ancient architecture. He wraps himself in a robe, sits comfortably with a newspaper, and soon reaches to ring a bell lying nearby. A servant hurries out and deposits a tray full of food upon the low table alongside the lounge chair, while his master gazes motionless off to the side. After the servant leaves, the man absentmindedly begins eating.

Our beggar remains crouched among the pines, waiting for the man to finish his meal. Only when the fork is finally put down does he decide to walk toward the gazebo. The man betrays no sign of astonishment when he sees the beggar. "You've made quite a killing in town, haven't you?" he inquires, while feigning to read his paper. The beggar, by now, has reached his side. "But not here," says the wealthy man, "not without working for it. I imagine you're now as rich as I." A wry smile crosses the beggar's holy face as he brandishes his charity box. The man continues. "I'll bet that each of your contributors is promised a handsome seat on high. So consider, old man, my sins, and the size of my fortune. How much must I pay for a box in the balcony?" With a smirk, he calmly folds his newspaper and turns to face the beggar for the first time, to find the charity box just inches away from his nose. "Stolen!" he screams, seized with sudden anger. "Every penny of it!"

"In the name of Heaven," says the beggar, unshaken, holding the box in front of the man's face, "insert a coin here, and it will be well with you."

The man lurches to his feet, arms flailing, and knocks the charity box to the ground. "Leave," he shouts, "or I'll have you removed at once, old Jew!" The two men's eyes meet, and the beggar dismisses an impulse to use some sort of power over the man, lest he forfeit his mission. He could paralyze him, as the mongoose does the cobra. As the man lets loose a stream of incomprehensible obscenities, the beggar steps back and begins mimicking his mad behavior, trembling wildly, then falling on all fours, yelping and growling and circling the man who thinks he is having delusions upon seeing the beggar transform himself into a dog! The dog barks, and the man panics and kicks it in the head, but the animal grabs the man's bathrobe and pulls so hard that the miser tumbles, head over heels, crashing to the ground.

"All right," the man whines, "I'll give you the money. But I am naked. I have nothing here." The dog attacks, his ferocity fired by the empty promise. Man and animal thrash about, knocking over the table, causing plates and dishes to shatter on the gazebo's marble floor. The man gropes pitiably among the fragments of glass and porcelain and the remnants of his meal. He reaches for a large bone and flings it across the lawn, beyond the pines. "Go get it!" he shouts to the dog that, good naturedly, goes scampering after the bone. It takes him seconds to find it, pick it up with his teeth, and run back to deposit it between the rich man's feet. The latter is delighted. He picks it up and readies himself to throw it again when suddenly cheers originating from a distance fill the quiescent air. The rich man raises up his eyes to discover hundreds of townspeople perched on the fence of his property. He waves to them, takes a step back and concentrates on throwing the bone a long way off. The cheers arise and are sustained, from the moment the dog runs after the bone until the moment it drops it at the rich man's feet. Cheers give way to shouts and applause, then laughter, mostly laughter. With every throw and every dog's run, the rich man attempts every elaborate way to throw the bone, forcing the dog to take a renewed tack to discover the place of the fall. It suffices to observe how the exuberant nature of the game so very little agrees with the rich man's bearing, to understand that he is having the greatest time of his life. The game would have lasted for a long time had it not been for the beggar's old age. This time around, instead of scampering after the bone, he stays in place, suddenly reverting to a standing position as the beggar in human form. And then, without warning, he goes over to the rich man and proceeds to twist his arm, literally, with the intent to bring him down to the ground. The rich man does nothing to resist the attack. On the contrary, he is the one who precipitates his own fall, after which the beggar begins kicking the rich man repeatedly with the back of his foot on the rib cage. The rich man screams for help. The townspeople stop laughing. Absolute silence is interrupted by scattered remarks directed at both the beggar and the rich man. Some people are protesting the beating. Others, on the contrary, are encouraging it, but soon the protests subside. No one has an inkling of what is really happening. What mostly confounds them is the fact that the rich man, who is taller and rather athletic, does little to defend himself against the elderly beggar. Even the manner of protecting his chest with his folded legs is contrived. The kicks are not truly kicks and the screams are not true screams either. It is a rehearsed drama between the two men who, moments before, were antagonists, but through the chemistry of their encounter are about to engender a love so deep as to render it contagious.

The townspeople are dumbfounded. It is a fight alright, but why does the rich man begin to laugh? They do not suspect that through this mock combat against the rich man, the beggar has engaged himself in inculcating them into some of the holy teachings of the Baal Shem Tov. Judging from their depressed spirit, acting with such foolishness was the only way that he could bring them back to life. Nothing else would have worked because the teachings are so deep they could not possibly have been taught in another manner. And if they could have been taught in a less dramatic way, they might have caused even the wisest among them to pass out. This demonstrates the extent of degeneration of their memory. The result of the episode was that no one reverted to his old self. The cure was complete.

The knowledge that the idiot shared with the writer, who in turn taught it to others who taught it to others throughout the world, became the paradigm of a new type of intellect. All the adepts mastered the use of the power of *equivalence*, meaning that they were all capable of substituting the tenuous nature of thought with purely material means. The result is so descriptive that it hardly lends itself to interpretation, for it skips over all rationale to alight directly upon the depths of the psyche where it is de-codified instantly. It does not end up as thought or imagery, but rather as an unyielding perception that outranks the finest of human expressions, and that is one of the most potent forms of memory—one that is fertilized by years of forgetfulness. All the senses seem to participate in the act of retrieval. Or perhaps, remembrance is so total because the senses swap roles. The ear hears ancient visions, whereas the eyes see the sounds of God's words.

On the feast of Purim, in the year 1971, I attended a Hasidic gathering with the Lubavitcher Rebbe. We were several thousand strong, all singing and clapping. I had come with a young man who, at that time, was confused about his beliefs. I stood in my usual place, a few feet to the right and behind the Rebbe. My guest stood right beside me. His face was flushed red, both from fear and guilt. He had the sort of wide opened blue eyes that seem to be continuously staring at an ardent source. After several hours, my legs and feet were hurting, and I felt a bit dizzy from lack of air. I was considering going outside for a break when, without warning, the Rebbe turned my way and looked me straight in the eyes. He placed two fingers against his mouth and nodded in my direction, several times. I could not understand what he meant. For every nod of the head, I responded with a shrug. His fingers still rested on his lower lip and he nodded once more, this time forcefully. The thought crossed my mind that he might have commanded me to whistle, but I dismissed it. Never would a man of his nobility ask for something so ludicrous. I looked over my shoulders to be sure that there was not someone else he was addressing, only to find that the people behind me were all looking at me. I turned to face the Rebbe again, thinking that if I did whistle, the Hasidim would throw me out of the place. I was not going to take risks. I was first going to mimic the whistling. I placed two fingers over my mouth and waited. The Rebbe's face lit up. This was it! I entered an unknown dimension as I blew my first whistle. The first blow was timid, but I quickly grew more self assured and went at it as forcefully as I could. Others soon joined until we were hundreds whistling. The air caught fire with the resonance of the piercing sounds. My lower lip ached from blisters. But the Rebbe would not let me pause. He was taking the matter quite seriously. He called for still more energy as I, in my abruptly unbound imagination, envisioned thick threatening black clouds shattering into dust. We discomfited darkness with our collective breath. Minds were swept clean of all indoctrination, and I knew my guest was being purged of his folly. Every sweet seduction murmured from the *other side* was blown away by the stiff wind we had summoned. Fallacious arguments flew away like frightened bats as we toned the walls of our hearts to prepare for an all-out war, fairly fought, wind against wind, challenging those irrational emotions that pose as thought, but whose essence is only wind. We alienated every gaseous enemy and incurred no casualties. Not even the singers hurt their throats as they sang background to our breath. Our final blast took off like the plaintive calls of a ram's horn. I was thinking of this as a folly ordained, a rehearsal for redemption, when the Rebbe paused.

It is four o'clock in the morning. I faintly hear the rising blare of the whistling in my head. I am thrilled by the idea that this could be a most ideal way to wage a war. No blood spilled. No need for retaliation. I am musing as evil forces attempt to drown me in their hideous noise. They know that the end is upon them, yet they give it a last try. I am so weary, but I have neither the will nor the strength to go lie in bed.

My imagination runs wild. I picture millions of people being led into a ten-ring circus, hung with fabrics of purple, blue and gold. Not all of the spectators have found their seats yet when it is announced that the Ten Commandments are about to be revealed in a physical form, one commandment for each ring. Some spectators are doing somersaults from excitement. I am sitting opposite the ring where the Second Commandment is being enacted. "You shall have no other gods before Me," announces a voice through a loudspeaker. We all stand up to applaud. Shortly after, we see false gods, sitting cross-legged in a circle, their eyes closed in what appears to me a gesture of penitence. By turns, they each confess the ways they have fooled us. They clap hands as myriads of adored deities materialize in the air. One god stands, and invites his audience to take potshots at the hovering objects, which shatter instantly when hit by the traditional rotten eggs and ripe tomatoes, or even by projectiles as small as sesame seeds. The most amazing sight of all is to watch deceptive thoughts zooming over our heads, bursting into flame with our mere intention to reach out and touch them. Small children lift their hands to grab them, popping them open between their chubby fingers. Some emit such a stench that many spectators rise to leave, but the gods drop to their knees, and plead with them to stay seated for the remainder of their show. The smell worsens each time a child pops open another god. Fearing a mass exodus, some of the gods hasten to dress in brightly colored baggy pants, clown makeup, and outsized shoes. As they leap and tumble in zany acrobatic display, the children pelt them with garbage, and the gods fight over the scraps, first as slapstick, then in dead earnest, when they realize this is their last meal. The scene unfolds in silence, with no music, no drums, no laughter.

In utter panic, the gods begin to disintegrate one by one, on their own, just trying to hold the crowd, and as they disappear in puffs of colored smoke, infants toddle in from all sides holding gold and silver bottles high above their heads, squirting sweet fragrances to offset the repulsive smell. Now the tight sound of trumpets pierces the confusion of the room, and the tambourines join in to ease the atmosphere with a mellow, shuffling beat. Flutes dust the air in rapid flurries. Expansive tones of stringed instruments gather lost and scattered notes, and bind them in full, firm measure. The audience shudders like tall grasses blown by a breeze. Time pulsates softly before turning pale, pale blue, while space suffers mild seizures from a sudden shift of structure, and the bellowing resonance of a ram's horn delays all existence in one quivering freeze.

It happened that, as I drowned
in the opaline blue eyes of the Rebbe, the
boundlessness of the infinite was revealed to
me in a glimpse. "Here is
a true man," I thought to myself, when his
head tilted to the side like
kindness and I lost consciousness.
I opened my eyes to find that I now
was in the presence of a king.

PART TWO

Playing with Marbles

The Vision

Of a Horse and Its Rider

The Night of the Just

WHERE A CHILD suddenly finds himself confronting growing pains and dealing with the constant fluctuations between being and nonbeing. He grows up trying to find ways to save himself from a rapidly disintegrating sense of reality. He searches for points of reference to stave off the bleeding and discovers the secure and limitless power of the deed. He finds his sanity through the *possible*. The possible becomes the norm which in the future will protect him against false prophets, even against his own dreams. * There follows a discussion on deciding which is worse: a life of pleasure or a life of total abstinence. * The chapter ends with a battle between the custodians of illusion and those of reality.

Playing With Marbles

VERYONE HAS his own particular rhythm, his own song. Everyone should find his own pace, thanks to which he will reach a good harbor. Pacing yields optimum speed. For while we tread on solid ground, the right pace will let us have a better grasp on the imaginary. My own pace has mainly consisted of walking along the road of the *possible*, to explore and abide by its configuration. It is there that I have met all my adventures. The approach is not new, because it is frankly Jewish.

The possible is a small, well-defined area, yet, it is there that the infinite comes to bloom. It is from there that the climb towards greatness begins, with whatever tool one chooses to lift oneself up, whether it be intellect, action, or the bold maneuvers of the *madness of the holy*. As we climb, we will find that the highest we can reach is no higher than the heavenly appointed measure of ourselves. Our goal is to get to that place.

My appreciation of the possible began at about the age of fourteen, but only my appreciation of it, not the practice, not at such an early age, when I could only observe it. I was the playful type. When I was not playing, I was dreaming. For life in the streets of Morocco was too vibrant to permit serious thinking.

In spite of that, however, a deeper meaning of existence began to form in my memory bank. It entered in stages. There was one particular event which touched off the whole process. It was in 1948, the year Moroccan Jews began to leave in large numbers for Israel. I had gone by myself on foot to a far-off bus station to say farewell to our favorite neighbors, a distinguished family. Both husband and wife occupied prominent positions in Jewish affairs. They were both righteous people. Even their two sons were little sages. My older brother and I were best friends with them. They spoke little and did much. There was a nasty war raging in Israel just then, and I thought that I might not see them again.

They were boarding the bus when I arrived. The sound of the ignition key left me lifeless. As I stood there, peering through the bus windows, watching them search for their seats, I was overcome with anguish. The noisy, too violent acceleration of the engine vibrated directly to my stomach. Soon the monstrous machine proceeded to leave the station and I walked beside it, waving to my friends until it turned at the first street. I followed it with my eyes until it disappeared behind the city wall.

That was when it happened. At that precise moment, I experienced a most devastating sensation. It felt as though I had been emptied out of existence. I remember how I went searching for a mirror, to take a look at myself. There was one just behind me. It had a pink hue to it. I made faces to myself to lend some tangibility to my presence. I made funny gestures to break myself away from the stillness of illusion, only to make things worse. The pastel tint of the mirror must have contributed to highlight my negative vision of reality. I felt pity for myself. I looked at my reflection, and my reflection looked back at me, and we both smiled, and agreed with each other that the good times had come to an end. Then I went back home.

There were days when these occurrences reached maddening intensities. One of the most unbearable feelings of all was to be confronted with the very improbable co-existence of the spoken word and the flesh. There was no way, as I saw it, that the physical body could formulate ideas or that the mouth could utter words. Reality was simply too good to be true. If I had ceased to exist at that moment, I would not have even noticed. There was not a day that passed by when I was not tossed between extremes. For years I lived in such a hell. It was pretty much the same routine. "I will close my eyes," I would say to myself, "and when I open them, the world will no longer be there." But it was always there, of course. It was reassuring, but only for a moment. For such positivity merely served to create a greater madness. There were times when the tossing about was so rough that it did not matter whether I was proven right or wrong. Whatever the outcome, it was most important that I put an end to the frightening ambiguity.

Perhaps the answer to the unsettling feeling may have been brought on by the anxiety of losing my friends. The truth, however, is that deep down I knew it had been with me for quite some time, only I had not paid much attention to it. Being the chronic dreamer that I was may have predisposed me to incur such a massive loss of reality. The fact is that from that day on, I became acutely disconcerted by the constant fluctuations between being and nonbeing. I had, until then, gone along with the idea that the world existed, but now I was not so naive. I knew better. Soon I found myself facing a dilemma. What was my moral obligation, to remain silent or to spell out the truth by telling people that they were living in an illusory world? And what if they thought me crazy? Therefore, I didn't tell anyone, even as it grew worse, when I found it unbearable to see people fade in and fade out of reality while conversing with them, or when I was unable to hear half their words. I would nod my head in approval, just to keep them going. Anyone who might have suspected anything must have probably thought that I had my head in the clouds. The sense of illusion was at times so overpowering that when I succeeded in breaking away from it, I would find myself bursting into the extreme opposite: an insufferable sense of the real. I could not tell which one was worse, so I kept running away from both. The only refuge I found was in sleep.

Most of my attention went into grounding myself. Vigilance made way for a more aggressive type of intelligence. Those back and forth trips between being and non being taught me to appreciate the dearness of existence more. As you may have already surmised, the experience proved to be the instrument of conditioning for my subsequent ceaseless quest for the possible. It also taught me that I had no vessel, and I was therefore inept at taking hazardous flights; no spiritual takeoff, and no mind-expanding drug either, not even alcohol. I was thinner than space. My principal preoccupation was to build intermediary stations between my precarious states of mind. If, in the future, I was to take a flight, I would first have to secure solid points of references within the real.

What I have just related is only part of the story. There was another incident that happened two years earlier, whose *denouement* exerted a great influence on my decision to adhere to the norms of the possible. We lived on a dead end street that was ideal for playing all sorts of games. There was no traffic. All of us had moments, in the various games we played, when we were down on our luck, or skill was lacking, and we would succumb to the temptation to cheat. None of us ever got away with it. We were all pretty sharp, and not easily fooled. Still, we would give it a try now and then. In my case, it was usually with marbles. The idea was to stand behind a line and shoot at a marble placed some six feet away. I had long arms and a tendency to lean forward, cutting the distance by half. My problem, however, was my older brother, who kept an eye peeled to catch cheaters like me in the act. He would threaten to break up the game if I ever tried such a scheme again. He was scrupulously moral, whereas for me it took tremendous effort to play by the rules. Under his watchful glare I would curb the urge and play for a few more minutes before finally quitting the game out of frustration and boredom.

On one such unlucky day I decided to try a new tack. While everyone else was pitching his marbles from the line, I took several steps backward and stood about fifteen feet from the target. I shot and missed. Just as I was about to try a second time, my brother loomed in front of me, grabbed me by the arm and dragged me back to the line. "Shoot from here," he snarled. "I know what you're thinking. If you miss from so far away, you've got the perfect excuse, and if you hit it only once, you're the champ. Just shoot from the line and don't be a wise guy."

I obeyed, and said nothing. What I should have said was that the game didn't interest me the way it was played. Though I was too intimidated to speak up, and the feeling was too vague to verbalize, I sensed that the target was somehow closer when I stood from afar, as if from that outrageous distance I established a kind of mystical rapport with the marble. It was a challenge that quickened my soul. Having stepped back from the mediocrity of the shooting line, I was more myself. Whether it was my impetuous nature or a sudden intuitive impulse that caused me to disregard all rationality, I sincerely believed I could span that impossible distance, and set a new standard, not only for my peers, but for all mankind.

My brother had me by the throat. I had no choice but to consent to come back to the shooting line. It took some time before I made peace with the idea of conforming to the rules, and once I did, I discovered during games how exciting it really was. Staying on the line opened doors. It gave new nuances to my imagination. Once I threw off my wings, I discovered how that line is where flight truly begins. From then on I never indulged in the impossible, almost. I made a few fugues, for I was not going to completely afflict myself with limitations at such a young age. I was trapped but I was also puzzled. I recall even enjoying living within the restrictions that I had imposed on myself, for they placed me in front of a keyhole through which I watched the human comedy. From such an observatory, I could tell who the true climbers were; who made it to the top and who did not. I could also tell who was truly righteous. The cheaters had one thing in common, they had plenty of shadows on their faces, and it was not difficult to discern a true revelation from a false one, for the latter fell flat on impact against one of my dreams. But even when a true one came along, I managed to keep a cool head. This is pretty much how I approached things, but remember that if I behaved that way, it was only attributable to the fact that I had a fragile vessel.

There is a story in the *Talmud* about the dispute between Rabbi Eliezer (the sage who was compared to a well in a previous chapter) and his colleagues, the subject of which has stirred so much discussion that it has become a central point in our tradition. There was a question as to whether a certain oven was considered pure or impure for cooking. Rabbi Eliezer was alone in holding the opinion that it was pure. Realizing that none of his arguments could convince his colleagues, he tried a new tack. He called for a heavenly revelation to help him make his case.

Pointing to a nearby carob tree, he said, "If the Law prevails as I say, let this carob tree prove it." And the tree was uprooted from the ground and flew two hundred yards away. The Sages were not impressed, but Rabbi Eliezer was not going to give up so easily. He turned to a spring that was flowing by and said, "Let this spring prove me right," and the waters began to run backwards. But that too had very little effect on his colleagues, who told him that it proved nothing. Then Rabbi Eliezer turned to the walls of the house of study and said, "Let these walls prove that the Law is my way." The walls tilted and were about to fall when one of the opponents, Rabbi Joshua, yelled at the walls, saying, "If scholars are arguing a point of law, what right have you to interfere?" It is said that out of respect for Rabbi Joshua the walls did not fall, but they did not straighten up either, out of respect for Rabbi Eliezer.

Rabbi Eliezer was not about to give up. He lifted his eyes and said, "Let the heavens proclaim that the Law is according to me!" Whereupon a Voice from Above was heard, saying, "Why do you quarrel with Rabbi Eliezer, whose opinion should prevail everywhere?" At that point, Rabbi Joshua, who was not in the least demurred, rose to his feet and said, "The Law is not in the heavens!" The heavens kept silent. The debate ended right there, but its repercussions have not abated. It is still giving rise to many commentaries, all of which express one fundamental precept: that the Torah is here to give us all the answers. And if it is here to make us wise, heavenly voices are not to interfere with our deliberations.

Some would think that Rabbi Joshua had a lot of nerve to address God the way he did, but don't let that worry you. Tradition has it that God took it well. The Talmud relates a few lines later how, when God was asked by Eliyahu the prophet how He had taken the rebuff, God answered, "My children have vanquished Me. They have vanquished Me!" This was an expression of endearment. God was overwhelmed, in the same way as a father is overwhelmed by a zealous son who is eager only to do his father's will. The son is so consumed by the desire to know his father that he carefully examines the books which his father likes to read. He meditates on every underlined word, makes various cross-examinations and annotations until the spirit of his father penetrates deeply inside him. He exults; for now he knows how to better serve him.

It is said that because he had dared go against the majority, Rabbi Eliezer was excommunicated (his excommunication lasted only one day) in spite of the fact that he was wiser than all of them. Being right, so it appears, was not enough to have him prevail. Truth was not at issue. The real issue was to decide what would be the safest manner to carry Jewish Law to its true port of destination: through the revelations of inspired individuals or through the more articulated decisions of an appointed court. They opted for the latter because they anticipated a time when the "Voice" would no longer speak. Except for Rabbi Joshua, who would later go to Rabbi Eliezer's grave to ask for forgiveness, they all died untimely deaths. But the Law was saved. If one wished to have an answer from God, one would have to do it primarily through the deed, the nerve center of the Law. The unassuming deed would lend definite credence to the answer. By giving the deed prominence, they pulled the rug out from under a horde of false prophets and ideologues. This was a revolutionary idea at the time, to give such a decisive role to the deed.

Every detail in that debate, when I first read it, thrilled me to bits. I identified with both Rabbi Joshua and Rabbi Eliezer. I followed the story with the strong sentiment that I already had it in my genes. It became my motto, even though I was far from eager to stick to the rules. Although I honored the Sages' decision, I was not yet ready to work for their cause. I toed the line in theory only, but if my actions were undisciplined, my dreams were not. I was a dreamer with a direction. I continued dreaming even when the idea of the possible matured. The growing man in me would not resolve to chase the child out. An agreement was drawn; one of the stipulations being that there would not be any compromise. Child and man would do as they pleased—no surveillance and no criticism from either side, and no obligatory meetings either. These would have to take place spontaneously. There was not only unity between the two, but complicity. The man made certain that the child's dream came true; whereas the child made certain that the man never compromised his highest goals. This type of concerted madness would later develop into my main instrument of war or peace. No one would know whose action it was, the man's or the child's.

Even less could they know what my next move would be. Nor would I. My ambivalent situation also served to guard me against taking myself too seriously. There was little chance of my being caught capitalizing on thoughts, with the idea of later doing business with them. This is, incidentally, how false religions are often born, with the infinite dreams and limited capacity of an adolescent mind.

But the great bonus of my dual existence was that it protected me against spiritual raiders: levitating gurus, wonder workers, or some power hungry psychics, who might come my way in the future. As powerful as their demonstrations would be, they could not affect me in the least, for these people made no weddings between extremes. They awakened no worthwhile memory in me. I was in no way influenced by the "wonders" wrought by the most sincere of them, some of them religious Jews, even when I saw truth in them. I had questions of anyone who could not comprise in his person both truth *and* legend. I would develop an instant allergy to those who did not unite thought and deed in their speech. My impatience with spiritual prodigies grew all the more intense as my observance of the deed grew more consistent. I made very little effort to judge situations, since the deed itself spotted every inconsistency for me. Or the deed would run so fast ahead, that in my effort to catch up with it, I would fall out of my dreams.

I t is our unpredictable nature, our fragility, that causes us to conform to the norms of the possible. Even the *Tzaddikim*, the Just, who are in no way incapacitated by the evil inclination as we are, have to conform to those norms. For the possible is a place where God's Will is most easily apprehensible, the only place where true greatness is obtained. There you can tell who is wise and who is merely a jobber of sorts, who holds his knowledge well, or who is addicted to it.

For as wise or knowledgeable as some people portray themselves to be, it remains to be seen whether they can truly affect the human spirit or simply excite it. There, in the confines of the possible, you can easily spot the unduly cautious: the greedy and conservative, who are in no way predisposed to take risks, and who therefore are very unlikely to sacrifice their possessions for a good cause. You can tell who is able to swim against the current; who has voluntarily tumbled down deep into the abyss, only to return a free man. For such was the entire *raison d'être* of the primordial breaking of the vessels: *to bring freedom of choice to the world.*

One other advantage of abiding by the possible's norms is that it enables us to contemplate the Divine from an ideal perspective. For acknowledging our true worth— not going beyond our situation, not playing righteous, not playing man, not simulating greatness through artifice—will render us adept at judging whether our spiritual flights or visions are fake or real. We will not go out of bounds so easily. We will not fall so low and so far as to confuse Jewish law with dogmatism. There is very little chance that we will give in to any type of cult. We will not, as did the Pharaohs and other cultish figures, before and after them, develop a bewitching fascination with the beyond. We should always choose life over death. We would spend an entire life building a separation, both in thought and deed, between reality and illusion. For when there is no clear delimitation between those two worlds, when all the borderlines are blurred, everything becomes permissible. The slightest contrary behavior would drain out the reality from its vessel, beginning with overindulgence, which is frankly repulsive, and its opposite, abstinence, which though at times commendable, may turn out to be as harmful to the spirit.

Those who overindulge in the pleasures of this world seem to be regulating the intensity of those pleasures in accordance with, and as prevention against, the void of illusion. They organize their calendar around their temptations. Time loses its abstract quality when they measure a day as one of so many laps away from the fulfillment of their desire, to such an extent that desire begins to look like life itself, that form supersedes essence, and forgetfulness supersedes memory. This, incidentally, could be the main cause for the pressing urge certain people have to go on indefinite cruises aboard ocean liners. They squander their past at each port. They consume their memory, walking the meandering narrow streets of forgotten villages. Theirs is an organized death. They die a little everywhere, but they die best in Egypt, where the shrine of Pharaoh's gold has a theistic effect on their inner void. The dramatic shape of the pyramid seems to indicate an exclusive claim on eternity, but from a distance it looks very much like a heap of debris. From the biblical point of view, it represents an extreme of materialism. With its wide solid base, that sits too well on the world, and its pointed summit, it looks as though it wants to tear heaven apart. It exhibits the unconscious death wish of the amnesiac visitor.

As for those who do away with reality through abstinence, one way or another, reality catches up with them. I have personally known or heard of quite a few teachers from the Far East, each one of them a master in his own discipline, who died from an excessive consumption of alcohol. In their active denial of the reality of this world, it is not surprising that they turned to spirits, whose semi-ethereal quality correlated aptly with the intangibility of their belief. Their belief was in their head only. Being all too human, they spent their last years burning their guts to feel the reality that they had so religiously attempted to deny.

It is the old battle between the custodians of illusion and those of reality. Ever since Creation, the champions of illusion have been trying every scheme under the sun to get dominion over the world, but the guardians of reality are resilient. They have every proof in hand to demonstrate that the immediacy of existence is both imperative and authentic. Now, both reality and illusion have formidable presence. Realizing that it cannot win, illusion cuts awesome figures over infinite space. Space is easily conquered, but it is time which suffers the greatest loss. Unlike space, time has no vessel with which it can make itself seen. Space, though conquered, at least has something to show for itself. It has the blue expanse of the sky to deflect anguish. Time, however, can be utterly spoiled. That is why, when reflecting upon his past, a person poor in deeds finds nothing but a void. His outlook on reality is bleak.

He says that he has not yet lived. He begs for some more years to try to have a more palpable grasp on reality. Meanwhile, the present is there to be declared real. Merchants in the marketplace scream prices behind baskets full of deeds, but the buyer is choosy. The world blinks from being to nonbeing, as the merchants hasten to advertise that deed is the only known good that *makes* time.

9

WHERE TWO immaterial doves appear in a vision before the eyes of a dismayed insomniac, and begin a series of utterly nonsensical dialogues between themselves that concludes with a revelatory secret word. * There follows a discussion on how the nature of a person decides the character of his vision. * The narrative then shifts to how a *Tzaddik* unites entities in his meditation, both in higher spheres and down here in this world. His thoughts are compared to birds that go on peaceful missions like Noah's doves. He stays awake to dispatch invisible messengers whose charge is to assist those in distress. The text continues with some observations on that dark force commonly called the *devil*, on a word he secretly holds, as well as on a promising aspect of memory.

THE VISION

NE NIGHT IN Sceaux, near Paris, France, in the year 1962, when I still lived in my parents' house, an uncommon event occurred. I decided to put what had happened that night aside, and not include it in these pages, when upon close scrutiny, it struck me that if I could turn things around, it would not confound the reader, as I thought it would. On the contrary, it might profit him. And so here it is, rendered as best I can. For lack of a better word, I have come to call what happened that night, a *vision*.

It was past midnight. I was lying in bed, suffering from sharp abdominal pains. Though I had put up with such afflictions more than once before, it had never been so excruciating. The pain spread quickly, even to the hands and feet. My entire body was one sore nerve. I could move my head, but only very carefully, or else convulsions would throb so hard that I could have lost consciousness.

Outside, the summer night was clear, and the moon almost full. Our neighbor upstairs, usually still active at that hour, had quieted down. I was left alone, illuminated by the light of the moon, under a shroud formed by clean white bed sheets. I looked at my disabled and emaciated body, and imagined the presence of death. I moved my head to make sure I was alive. A spasm of unbearable intensity shot through my spine, cutting off my breath. I groaned, and one of my brothers who shared the room with me asked if he could do anything to help. I answered somewhat impatiently that I was having my usual bellyache. That was all I said.

I was trying to put myself to sleep when it occurred. Something inside me began to stir. To this day, I still do not know for sure what it was. I paid little attention to it, concentrating instead on my pain and my need to sleep. But the force inside me was, I dare say, much too conspicuous to be simply ignored. It insisted on making itself known.

It was without form, yet it moved onward, outside myself and close by, perhaps two feet away from my nose. I was so stunned by its beauty and its abstract reality that I forgot my pain. Its presence made my own being seem exceedingly gross by comparison. I was only a shell in which it happened to live. It went back inside of me, and then out again, several times, as though enjoying the change of atmosphere. The first thing I noticed was that it was of superior intelligence. Don't ask how I knew. That was just the way I understood it. As I said, it had no form. Had it resembled anything, I would venture to say that it looked like an incorporeal dove.

It went inside me once more for a short while, and when it came out, as it floated leisurely before my face, there suddenly emerged from somewhere, another dove. This one was similar to the first, but it could have been older, and perhaps slightly larger, and more experienced. They chattered like birds, excited to have met. They talked too quickly to be understood, chirping with a joy that rushed out faster than their words.

They might have been two sisters who had not seen each other for some time. The second one, the visitor, was definitely wiser and held a higher rank, and had apparently come to draw up a periodic report. The younger one briefed her about some of her earthly adventures. After each topic they kissed, as if drinking a toast.

They acted as though I was not there, mocking my sluggish mind with a friendly insolence. I could not help thinking that I had once known their language, until they began to speak at a much higher speed, something that made me realize how their first exchange had been mere social patter. Now it seemed to me that the structure of their sentences had been put in reverse order, yet remained curiously correct. They spoke in rapid-fire patter. I could make nothing of it, but I knew that whatever they were saying was of a prodigious intelligence, beyond human grasp.

None of it made sense, except that at the end of each exchange a *word* was clearly pronounced. I strained to hear it. When they decided to stop, I pressed them on to further dialogue. At my urging they babbled on in the same irrational order, making use of that same impossible, nonchalant intelligence that souls must employ when they are freed. When the *word* was pronounced again, it struck me that I was being provided with something that could save the entire world.

It was a simple little word. I thought to myself, I will go out of here and scream it aloud. It was going to fire all minds, before it brought peace on earth. I knew I had to write it down, before I lost it, but I could not get out of bed because I was completely paralyzed.

I was overcome with another series of spasms. My brother heard me groaning, and this time insisted on giving me some help. I assured him that I was quite all right, quickly brushing him off for fear of losing my two companions. Luckily, they were still there. I invited them to resume their frenzied chattering, and they obliged without hesitation. I exhorted them to keep on with it, in the hope that the *word* would be carried through to the break of day. They pronounced it several times. It was a word of pure irrefutable logic, irresistible even to the narrowest of minds, but unfortunately I blew it, because I dozed off. When I came back to myself, the doves were gone, and with them the *word*. I was left empty and anguished, groaning in pain. A few moments later it was dawn.

I was devastated. I felt like a carcass. My essence had left me. The *word* became an obsession. Even years afterward, I began a novel in an earnest attempt to track it down. I believed I would be able to fence it in the way one fences in a horse. My own words would be the bait, like trained thoroughbreds prancing in the field to lure the wild mare into the corral. Thus entrapped, unspoken, but hovering over the expanse of the text, the *word* would gradually and imperceptibly give itself to the reader, who would never be the same.

The novel never saw the light of day. There was one third left to go when I got involved in concocting natural recipes and medicines. I ended up writing books on physical health instead. There was no sense of conflict about it whatsoever. It was the wisest thing to do. People's health came first. The unfinished novel is sitting in some drawer. I keep it as a souvenir.

Long after the episode with the doves took place, I related it to one of my brothers, only to hear him tell me offhandedly that something similar had also happened to him, but under different circumstances: There was no pain and no doves, therefore no dialogue, but the incessant pronouncement of an indistinct word that seemed to answer all existential queries. The revelation left me quite puzzled. I wavered between being happy for my brother and mourning over the fact that the vision was not such a unique experience after all. The good thing about it, however, was that it took quite a bit of weight off of my mind. I was no longer the exclusive possessor of a secret word, because what happened to my brother could have been experienced by others as well. This helped me to let go of it. But for years, it would, every so often, come back to haunt me, until I began to feel guilty for allowing such a beautiful experience to go to waste. Downplaying it, I believed, was tantamount to sinning. Therefore I decided to put it on paper. Writing would either demystify it or give it justice. I would let the page be the judge.

The first thing I learned was that the vision was not a haphazard event. Somehow, I was the right person for it, precisely because I was an unfit recipient. In other words, it was the nature of my vessel that decided the character of the vision. Incomplete or distorted, the vision taught me at least one thing: it made me discover new inroads to memory, which, until then, I had merely approached through standard means. I am speaking of a type of memory that is shaped according to the fitness and purity of the vessel.

It was no coincidence that the vision occurred while I was paralyzed, to let me know who I am: a partial cripple, who nonetheless cannot use his deficiency as an excuse. It compelled me to learn how to chase after big game with small means. And, it confirmed that my salvation would be to keep in line with the road that had been traced for me.

What was I to do? What do you do when you lose a revelatory thought? Wouldn't you try every possible means at your disposal to recapture it, such as retracing your steps to reconstitute whatever was said or done before or after the thought was formed or announced? The truth, however, is that so long as your capacity is lacking, your deeds are unable to call the lost thought back. It will elude you, which most likely means you do not deserve it. It does not wish to be in bad company. You may be sufficiently sharp-witted to formulate it, but you are not a good enough host to hold it. You happen to have a quick intellect that towers over an ill-equipped body.

This is how incomplete or blurred visions occur, by way of chemical interaction, when those visitations are brought about by the difference of potential between our condition and the real world; only we pay very little attention to those delicate imprints. This is where most of us are holding, and it matters little whether one person is more keen in perceiving those visions than another or not. The truth of the matter is that all of us belong in the same basket, with the exception of Moses and the Just. Moses had no such visions. He saw things the way they really are, because there was no difference in potential between his being and Heaven's demands of him. He did not interpret what he saw. He did not dream, since dreams are drawn out of the gray area that exists between subjective and objective realities. In his descriptions of the real world, he had no need for allegories since he nourished himself at the very source of memory. It is the same with the Just, who respond to the world from spiritual fullness. The gift of remembrance that allows them to retain a permanent hold on everything they learn, see or hear, could only come from their deeds. Entrust them with a passage from Scripture and they will return it to you with a new life to it. Their memory is dynamic. You give them grapes, they give you wine. You entrust them with a dream of youth, and they make a man out of you. Their presence redeems all the days of your past. Their cup runs over.

If, as was explained earlier, most visions are ignited from a friction of two realities—our own, against that of the real world—then mine could only have been ignited by a difference of potential as well, inasmuch as I was not practicing too many *mitzvot* at the time. Yet, in spite of my not deserving it, it happened. I would say that it was a pure moment of grace. If that is the case, then why capitalize on it by making it public? One simply does not take credit for something one does not deserve in the first place. My brother had kept his vision to himself, as many others, I presume, have done. But I had other plans. I wanted to take a crack at the myth of visions, explain how they basically originate more from deficiency than saintliness; and then making an about-face, take another crack at deciphering what Divine Providence had tried to tell me in the form of my own vision. While I may have the right to deny truthfulness to a vision, I may not deny the existence of Providence's constant flow of communiqués that animate my being. For is not the reality of my existence, and everything around me, woven by the crisscrossing of those communiqués? Aren't we made and continually sustained, as it is said in the esoteric texts, by a combination of the holy letters of the *Aleph Bet?*

Would it not be enthralling to one day have an artist of great insight and sensitivity capture these heavenly communiqués on canvas? I dare submit for such a tableau that memory be painted with streaks of green, and that imagination run parallel to memory, with the difference being that its streaks are broken and of a lighter color. Kindness, which occupies most of the background, would have to be white, with shades of lilac and lavender, which, in certain places, would turn to cardinal red, the color of might, or severity. And then, in a stroke of true genius, the painter would set our minds astir with colorful patches exploding here and there, in place of human potential. Imagine writers, storytellers, or musicians, attempting to do the same, each one in his respective discipline. We would have no need of visionaries to read Heaven's writing for us, of course, the condition being that we would have previously gained the humility it takes to perceive these writings. In occupying very little space, humility makes it easy for Divine Providence to manifest itself, whereas vanity, with its raised chest, is blind to all those providential writings. It looks for visions instead, and finds them, to wrap up hastily in murky and deceiving metaphors.

Twenty-five years, filled with adventures and encounters with various people whose personae interblended so perfectly with the legendary, have altered my perception of the vision. Included in those twenty-five years are studies of both exoteric and esoteric literature, and of the practice of unglorified deeds. If my perspective of the vision has changed, none of its components were renounced, except for the *word*, which no longer lures me as it once did. The doves' maddening talk, on the other hand, has turned out to be a spirited and practical model that serves to assess the degree of truthfulness in speech. As for their immaterial presence, it has surprisingly been made somewhat more acceptable, I find, by the fortuitous combination of the practiced deed, and the transparent, nearly immaterial being of the *Tzaddik*. You might discover, should you be privileged to have a meeting with such a person, whose light presence can be compared to that of an angel, how time loses its preeminence. You disappear into infinite space. You take wing. You lose your mind from excess joy and start speaking nonsense. Try as you may, words come out jammed in your mouth. But the *Tzaddik*, the Just, does not mind. As a matter of fact, he could be encouraging it. For the first time in your life, it is only you who speaks, and nobody else. For the first time in your life you can hear your true voice. You go out in the streets with your head burning, speaking with madness, faster than you could have imagined, and you go in reverse, yet still manage to make terrific sense to the soul. Your voice becomes the mouthpiece for Divine Providence. You make immaterial, yet enduring, contact with people whose depressed lives hang in thin air. You fly above and between their split minds, and unite it all into one clear thought. Meanwhile, people with "routinized" intellect can only object to your unintelligible speech. You can't explain that the *Tzaddik* himself is the direct source of your incoherence. Neither can you explain how, while in his presence, you could not be as attentive to his words as to his incredible reality; and how, coming out of there, fever blows away every pocket of vanity. All you take with you is a resolution, or a rhythm, that prompts you to transmit the unspeakable. You compensate thought with noise. You sound like a chirping bird. You make no sense whatsoever. At the end of your incoherent discourse, a redeeming word is clearly heard deep inside the heart of the listener.

AFTERTHOUGHT.
A later attempt to recapture the vision.

There I was, lying lifeless in my bed, trying to find some sleep, with pain forbidding the slightest body movement. If my body was wasted, my head had never been so alive. A myriad of thoughts were hitting me from all sides. All of them were pure. None were evil, probably due to the fact that my body was no longer connected to my head. I was righteous by default. Being all brain represented some risk, though, in the sense that, in not being supported by the body, the brain would dry out. It would become so irreducibly intellectual, and there would come a time when it would not be able to speak the truth. I was so feeble, my soul could easily have stepped out of me, but I do not imagine that it would have had the imprudence to venture too far away from me. Instead, it had to dutifully remain at close proximity to guard my breathing. Although it is pertinent to say that a soul could do everything it pleases after it is no longer confined to the body, I would not stretch that so much and so far as saying that it would evaporate out of me, escape like steam, or, as would have been my case, fly out of me in the tangible form of a dove.

Lately, I have come to terms with the idea that the dove in question might have been a reflection of my frail existence, a mental projection of the best in me, my essence, that wanted to leave out of impatience or boredom, from having been caged inside a body that apparently did not deserve to be its host. This is as realistic an explanation as I can imagine. Still, that would not get me too far inasmuch as I have a second dove to contend with. As far as this one is concerned, I have no explanation for it, none whatsoever. But that difficulty arises only when I consider the doves as separate entities. In that framework, I become inordinately dogmatic and too analytical for my own good. It takes me nowhere, when deep inside I know I can gain some real benefit from it. However, it is totally different when I look at the doves as one unit. Together, they happen to support each other's probability of existence. Whereas one dove alone brings doubt and illusion, the two together weave reality. The rule of thumb is that when you have doubt about the existence of something, the testimony of two witnesses can make that thing real. With my faith in Divine Providence restored, I find myself inclined to take risks to the point of proclaiming that the appearance of the night visitors was not only real, but necessary to my growth.

Thus heartened, I can now put all rationale aside to make contacts that do not require any proof or development, because the heart understands. I wish, just for a moment, I could afford the liberty to think dangerously, to think of nothing, and not be bound by the obligation to explain each step. I want to go for it, not knowing what there is to discover, nor having an ulterior motive for taking that liberty. I do it because it has become a necessity of life to unite the disunited, in the same manner that birds instinctively join their wills with a quick kiss. It is my own poor way of trying to emulate the esoteric unions or *yihudim*, which the Just, in their wisdom, make between holy entities in the higher spheres.

Whereas I unite noises and forms and words to save the day, the Just unites worlds. When I am prevented from uniting my own thoughts, he unites his soul with mine, with one word, or one look. If distance should separate us, he does it through a messenger. With every thought and situation carefully pondered, I would tend to believe that the meeting of the two doves was nothing less than one of those *yihudim*, one that was, in all probability, made by someone entrusted with the unique power to make contact with the lost sheep— a Just, naturally.

But who was he?

I have before my eyes the distinct image of one such saintly person seated at his desk. He faces an open window. He regularly posts himself there at a fixed hour of the night, dispatching life-giving thoughts to those in need. These thoughts arrive wherever he wills them to arrive, no matter what. The effect they have on the recipient's life attests to the eminence of the point of origin. This saintly person, as it happens, is none other than the commanding *Tzaddik* of his generation, whose soul comprises all souls. I would not be overstretching things too much by saying that it was one of those dispatched thoughts which reached me that fateful night, to set my life in order, and specifically to present me with a language that the mystics call the *"madness of the holy."* It also taught me, in retrospect, that the object of remembrance that we ardently seek is not necessarily as vital as the action that leads to it, thus urging me to raise form to the level of essence, until essence, which I cannot always obtain through the effort of my intellect, enters the marrow of my bones. I would be wise and never know it. I would, if it is at all feasible, identify with my actions to a point where I would behave like the two birds. As thoughtless and as carefree as they seem to be, they were still just as capable of giving rise to redeeming thoughts in people's heads.

Should not this total identification with action, this loss of self, be the benchmark of true greatness? Would not that be the only way for the vain to redeem themselves? Would not people's inflated ego at long last experience true joy, in view of the fact that true joy can only be obtained when the self gets utterly lost in the action? The same should be true for wisdom. What about memory? To what extent is it affected by vanity? And while we are at it, why not go for bigger fish by asking that question about the devil himself? Let us suppose that, just like everyone else, he too is endowed with the gift of memory. Could he then be redeemed, since, as was explained, memory is redemption? Is it pure coincidence that a week earlier I was told something that relates perfectly to that subject? According to the Baal Shem Tov, the devil would apparently be in possession of a word that could put an end to all human suffering, but he hides it so jealously that no one has so far been able to steal it from him. Two distinct thoughts struck my mind when I heard that. The first was that if the devil only possesses the word, he does not necessarily remember it or understand it. He is a salesman who knows practically nothing about a certain item that he has had for quite some time on a shelf.

The second thought was even more revealing. It struck me all the more since it was familiar to me. A day or two went by before I discovered the reason for my irrational manner of approval. In recounting the adventures of his youth, my father had given us, all his children, an answer, as we spent long hours riveted to his words. While still in his early teens, my father had led caravans, complete with camels and mules, across the vast empty spaces of Morocco. It was not infrequent, that while crossing certain regions which were abundant with mountain thieves, he had to seek refuge with none other than the chief brigand himself, with the express intent of entrusting him with his own money. Imagine what a brilliant stratagem that was, going directly to the enemy and seeking asylum. Because the honor of the chief brigand was paramount, it was out of the question that he, as host and trustee, would appropriate the money for himself. Who would have then dared attack the guest? The chief brigand would have been only too proud to defend him. Those were the rules.

But one thing still remains unresolved. Where did my father learn to use this stratagem? His father, who before him had also driven caravans through every desert road of the country, must have passed it on to him. It could only have been passed on this way. If not by his father, then by his grandfather. Suddenly it occurred to me that I had chanced upon an aspect of memory which is not so much an act of remembrance as it is a cognizance of something already known. Here, the soul knows secrets from herself, none of which, however, would be disclosed until she met the mate in whose contact she would be prompted to speak the ineffable. Aside from the usual excitement, normally brought on by the meeting of two friends, there are no signs which augur that something uncommon is in the making. In reality, though, joy—this one born out of the anticipation to participate in the creation of a new intelligence—implodes with the silent vigor of spring, in bodies that have readied themselves for the seed they will fecundate. As surely as water mirrors the image of the face, so joy, which runs fluidly in the veins, sets astir ancient knowledge in furtive visions.

10

T HE TEXT OPENS with a discussion about people who mistake a dog for its master, and other delusions of that sort, such as how the false often presents itself ahead of the true. * There follow a few comments on the forces that have replaced the false gods: the new seers, the clairvoyants, the psychics, the second-class mediums, the channelers, and the gurus with double-breasted suits. * There are some pertinent observations on how the guest comes to protect his host against these fix-all healers. * There are a few daring remarks about how the observant Jew has very little use for *balance*. * The text concludes with a story about a wounded rider who is saved by his horse.

OF A HORSE AND ITS RIDER

BSERVE A DOG in the company of its master. Having been with him for so long, it feels free to run ahead, or lag behind. It knows its master's path. It rolls and scampers across lawns like a puppy each time the thought of its master's love crosses its uncomplicated brain. Watching it frolic, the downhearted or the lonely grow envious of the animal. They think it is favored, that it has grace. And upon seeing the dog turn the street corner far ahead of the man, one might come to imagine that the dog is, in fact, the master, for it is leading the man.

Now consider this: it often happens that the false presents itself moments ahead of the true and then it fools you. My own annals about the phenomenon are cluttered with examples, some of which concern surprise encounters with long forgotten acquaintances.

More than once, during walks in my own town or during my travels, I have spotted a familiar face from some distance away. I hasten my steps, and improvise gestures to attract his attention. I even shout his name. He throws a quick look in my direction, and seems not to recognize me, even as he includes me in his expressionless gaze. Coming closer, I smile and say his name again, only to receive a glazed look in return. I realize I have made a terrible mistake. The man only happens to bear a striking resemblance to the original. After mumbling an apology, I walk on.

Suddenly, from around the corner, the original himself emerges, in the flesh, saluting, grinning, and calling my name. Now I am the one who fails to react. My natural emotions have been squelched by the abortive meeting with his double. Not until he embraces me do I accept the fact that it is really *him*.

This world is rife with ghostly symmetries born of illicit rendezvous between truth and falsehood. The trickster captures a mirror image of reality reflected from the source, and rushes it to market before it can vanish. The merchandise has to move quickly, because ersatz truth cannot be held for very long in greasy hands. The vendor sells at a low markup, in big volume. He turns a nice profit, and makes a name for himself. And when, moments later, the long-awaited visitor arrives with the genuine article, he finds an indolent populace that is already sated.

The long-awaited visitor, who is a redeemer in his own right, is definitely unexpected. Therefore, he is unwanted. He would like to tell them that they will not reap any benefit from the stolen merchandise. Other than the pride of possessing a prize object, they will find that they can enjoy none of the object's virtues. But, as often happens, they will not pay attention to his words. This is their lot, and their folly, they say, without a trace of regret. They display the same type of madness as those who dare try to possess the holy city of Jerusalem. The adulterers! They lust for her in the same way that they lust for one more woman for their harem. What do they see in her that they want to possess? What do they know about her true worth? I have prayed to be united with her ever since I can remember. She is my sister, my wife. Yet boorish men, Don Juans with lewd speech, are at each other's throats over who is going to get her first. I despise their vicious advances. I have been living in fear that they would defile her. What would become of me if that ever happened?

Meanwhile, day after day, I have been sending word that I will soon be reunited with her, and she has constantly answered that she has everything ready for my return. She is revealing so many secrets to me. She tells me what the boorish men murmur when courting her, the crude language that they use. When they see that it gets them nowhere, they invariably grab whatever they can of her garments. This one takes her kerchief, another one her bracelet, or an earring, or the pin that gathers her hair. Then they boast that she has given them souvenirs.

Except for a few lapses due to its inborn animal instinct, the dog has a basically gentle nature. To cite just one example, it is not ashamed, even before its master's eyes, to ease itself on trees. This dual character has bled over into a global psyche. It has made it easy for fundamental deists to become devout believers, as it has become easy for those who hold noticeably saintly positions to turn to the side and opportunely scratch their itch, then casually go on with the business of orchestrating their followers' devotions. These people have the same glabrous faces as the statuettes they worship, serenities of bronze, clean shaven to death, so ambivalent that there ought to be a law that forbids glimpsing their deadly demeanor.

Aside from that, there is very little else to fear. All false gods have perished. The war is virtually ended. There are only a few skirmishes breaking out here and there, a handful of petty thieves taking advantage of the relaxed surveillance. Most of them, however, mean no harm. These are second-class mediums and psychics, the new seers, whose powers are appropriately given to them to cater to those who find it confining to conform to the norms of the possible. This sort of malaise was never more evident than in the 1960s, when the youth flew too quickly in every direction, and by every available means. Desire looked very much like life, and death was the ultimate adventure. Love was in the air. Music, gurus, and drugs were sending nearly everyone to cosmic space. People flew in droves and came down in droves. On seeing the hecatomb, I lost my appetite for adventure. I aged before my time. I became practical in trying to figure out ways to intercept their falls and nurse their wounds.

Here, in passing, is a brief summary of one of those casualties. It happened in California in the year 1969, at Big Sur, where I had gone for the summer to give a few talks on natural healing. After one of the talks, a man took me aside to tell me that his wife had died five years earlier, and that he had not known a decent night's sleep since. He had just informed her that he was leaving her for another woman, and he had gone to the bedroom to pack his belongings. Not more than a few moments had passed before he heard a loud detonation. He ran to find his wife staggering, her head covered with blood. She died in his arms, staring at him.

Since then, he said, he had not had a single moment of peace. The little sleep he did get brought only nightmares. Her ghost haunted him continuously. His despair drove him to seek counsel from clairvoyants in the hope of finding some way to obtain his wife's forgiveness. The advice he was given was almost always the same: that he would have to try to contact her spirit. Ideally, said one guru, it should occur on the exact same day in the month in which she had taken her life, preferably in solitude, in the woods. So month after month, he roamed silent forests, performing ghoulish invocations. When he began to feel uncomfortable with these practices, he followed someone else's suggestion that he build her a shrine, where he brought her a peace offering every day after dawn. But nothing worked. He tried all sorts of meditations, all in vain. This was where it stood when we met.

All the while as he spoke, we had been walking in an open field. I stopped and said that there were not two ways to solve his problem, only one. I asked if he was ready to put my advice into practice. When he assured me that he was, I wasted no time in replying point blank that he had to go back to the place where he had faltered, which meant, finding himself a wife. Only this time, I emphasized that he should be faithful to her, but he did not seem to like that one bit. I could hear him thinking: "I knocked at the wrong door; this one is a purist." While I thought, "This one is going back to more clairvoyants and more gurus, until he exhausts every one of them." We spoke a few minutes more, he thanked me, and we parted ways. I never saw him or heard of him since.

But I never forgot him. Did my words have some influence on him? Judging from his reaction, I doubt they did any good. I only hope that in my pointing out a very precise manner of cure, I had not been instrumental in confusing him even more. But one thing is certain. At the time we met, the true meaning of life had so much slipped away from him, he was ripe for joining a cult. In the 1960s, this was a classical procedure: to excuse one's aberrant desires with the practice of chimerical communions with the unknown. It's a perennial trick to turn one's weakness, one's ineptness to confront desire, into power, into the fabrication of a religion. In the 1960s, it was more obvious, when streets were communal living rooms. It is still not an uncommon thing to meet with people whose spirituality is mostly obtained from such a reversal, who fabricate their own dimension and declare it real. They become meek, all in good faith. They bathe in mud and show clean hands. They are like camels. They chew their cud while holding their heads high, even as their unsplit hooves conceal great lies. Yet, in spite of this, truth passes through their fingers. The answer to why God permits such desecration of the spirit is simple. It is in the nature of truth to unconditionally give of itself. Even when stolen, it remains indivisible. Throughout history, it has been lending grace to the dual spirit of its captors. No wonder the attention is on them. How are we then supposed to prove that truth is not on their side?

Illusion often manages to speak first, revealing nothing of the truth that time, which it likes to conquer, owes its existence to the exercise of the mitzvah. For, if movement from one point to another in space creates time, it behooves one to consider that, thanks to its perpetual journeying between heaven and earth, the mitzvah must, of necessity, be securing the permanence of the world.

In practical terms, it means that we should open our home to guests. We ought to declare our house an open house, and come to appreciate how much the deed of hospitality improves our vision of the world. Guests can do more to change a person's character than does will. Nothing but a steady flow of guests, mostly unannounced and informal, will make a dent on such social evils as greed for material possessions.

Guests also make you immune to other evils, and contrived social civilities that devour your essence. Guests can rid you of self-importance and a false sense of honor— or the opposite, any vile behavior that has you overextend your hand and bow your head before the socially privileged. Honor is put in its right place. Everyone is made equal under your roof. Vanity becomes as conspicuous as a rotten tooth. You manage to retain all your candor; your alertness of mind alternates with your open-heartedness. Therefore, you do not judge as supernatural the fact that you can effortlessly anticipate the schemes of those who intend to trick you, whether their expression is frankly evil or restrained. Seeing the perpetrators of these schemes at work is like watching well-trained animals performing difficult acrobatics. At times they are so good at it, you catch yourself applauding. Their accomplishments are a far cry from the days when people would actually walk on water or fly in the air, but their powers are nonetheless impressive enough to cause some damage to our freedom of will. The list includes, to name but a few, the sleep talkers, those mediums who make stark revelation during self-induced sleep, and the channelers who summon the spirit of the dead, and even the most benign clairvoyant. All of these, whether they will admit it or not, tamper with the nature of the spirit to the point of squeezing it down to a mere commodity. Because the sort of spirit they invoke responds to them, they come to deal with the heavens irreverently. Eventually, spirit becomes synonymous with energy. This confined approach to worship must, of necessity, cause the heart and the mouth to forget how to pray to God. Here, bliss is received through perfectly rehearsed body postures. Meanwhile, the heart is dead, even as the mind meditates on unity.

Furthermore, aside from sparing one the humiliation of subjecting oneself to any of these inferior aspects of worship, a hospitable house opens one to the more legitimate aspects of the spirit. An open house will take the edge off an overwhelming miracle by putting it in a more manageable perspective. Each demand of the host, each preoccupation with his guests, creates an entirely new wisdom which alters the too persuasive and enchanting nature of the miracle. For is there a greater blessing than having the ability to solve life's puzzles by the command of one's thoughts? And is there a more opportune occasion for the soul than being able to participate in the imparting of thought, and seeing that it falls in line with its corresponding action?

From one day to the next, you find yourself flying high with your homegrown wisdom. Your house is your ship. From your vantage point, many factions, and most of what they stand for, seem like cartoonish renditions of truth. Many fine scholarly opinions turn surprisingly fetishist. Praise is offensive to your liver. You vomit honor like phlegm. The remembrance of the faces of your guests makes such an imprint on your eyes that you become visually immune to coercion. Each face becomes a purifying thought. Now imagine that in the midst of such an impending vision, the translucent presence of the *Tzaddik*, your teacher and master, emerges between all the faces. His face appears as the sum of all the faces, or better yet, their equivalence. He has come to protect you, in the same manner that Jacob protected his son Joseph by appearing before him in a vision. What sort of evil would dare harm you while your master is beside you? You are sheltered inside of his thoughts. You are actually riding inside the space of a thought that was released moments ago, or perhaps years earlier, in anticipation of your perilous journey. From now on, you base all your operations and speak your mind from there. Thus, voluntarily bound, you find yourself spontaneously working wonders with a pure breath that you exhale out from the holy mouth of your master.

In the same way that the seer is tied up with his gift of prophecy and vision, I am tied up in the possible. My redemption is there, not elsewhere. When the light dims for me, I pay the *Tzaddik* a visit to be reassured in my faith that the possible is the most scenic road. I get from him the boldness with which to reach further in the journey. He gives me a song, a cadenced thought, that beats continuously in my ears, whispering to me words that keep my pace steady. At times, the song becomes a battle cry in my head. The *other side*, the common enemy of all humanity, ululates like a hyena each time it hears it. The angel of doubt is, all at once, dumbfounded, whereas indecision, the most devastating of all negative forces, stands at attention. Sweet and enticing nostalgia, an offshoot of indecision, has swallowed its perfidious tongue. The legitimate need or desire for peace and quiet, for a house with trees in a lost place, has altogether left me. As of now, my only wish is to stare at the silent and dark blue night of Jerusalem.

I t once happened, in the midst of a talk a Hasid was giving at our house, that one of the listeners interrupted him to ask a question which was irrelevant to the subject at hand. "What is intuition?" he asked. The Hasid appeared puzzled. "I never heard of that word," he said. Someone immediately volunteered to explain to the Hasid what intuition meant. Another, decidedly alarmed, inquired whether intuition has an equivalent Hasidic expression. Someone made sincere attempts at trying to locate where the equivalence could possibly be found. More such reflections were thrown at the Hasid, who kept insisting that he did not understand what they were trying to say. The original questioner was by now beside himself. "Aren't you, by any chance, putting us on? Intuition is a household word," he said. "It's a heavenly gift that transcends all forms of intelligence," said another.

The Hasid was young, articulate, American born, with a fairly good command of the English language. This was not a simple case of semantics. How could he not have known about intuition? The discussion was growing even more heated when it dawned on me that perhaps we Jews have no intuition! I was transported. Why hadn't I thought of it before? But how was I to prove it? It came, at first, as an insight. Then it became a certainty. I recall having had the secret pleasure of wanting to shock everyone present with the news. I might have said something to the effect that intuition is not something vital to the Jew, that he doesn't have to rely on it. To him, it is more like a vestigial faculty that he uses for his own survival. By contrast, others have to dip into the universal pool, and therefore must resort to that faculty. The jungle forces them to hatch that egg. In my capacity as host, and in my sudden awareness of having interfered with the Hasid's train of thought, I invited the latter to resume his talk.

As years went by, I made further forays on the subject, and discovered that the split between Jacob and his brother Esau resides, on the whole, in the difference of approach to decision making. It is an ongoing dispute between the thinker and the intuitive. To put it bluntly, it boils down to whether or not one includes God in his thinking.

Let us use the classical example of the fork in the road, before which we would place two people, each with his own type of belief, to see how they will choose. There is a great deal at stake here. Chances are that the intuitive type will first go through an extended period of meditating and fasting to clear his vision. He will stay put until he becomes acutely sensitive to every cosmic pulsation, to the point of making himself one with the world, following which his whole being will be naturally drawn to its desired destination. He may even consciously remove God from his thoughts. In such a manner, he can claim the verifiable fact that all decisions are his will. His achievements, the unique manner with which he passes obstacles, or remedies past mistakes, testify to the fact that he is the sole captain of his ship. His machine is so well attuned to both the natural and the social environment that every motion on his part—the effect brought on by the meeting of his person and the outside world—explodes in your face like a miracle. However, beware. If he is not very well prepared, then the slightest error, one bad digestion or an incomplete meditation, will cost lives. If such is the case, the remedy is invariably the same: when the intuition is not good enough, sharpen it to the hilt, to dwarf any chance of misfortune. The intuitive type is an individualist. He is apt to either redeem the world around him or destroy it.

By contrast, the decision taken by the opposite type has its source in intelligence. It happens so quickly that it could be mistaken for intuition. It seems that no thought process is involved, when in truth, what appears to be a one track communiqué is actually a composite of forces instantly assembled by the mind. It is an editing of things learned or experienced. Opinions of sages are voiced from the actual present back to Sinai. It is having a small court in one's head, for much is at stake. All evidence is gathered before a final judgment is pronounced. The search is actually a work of memory. Here the humble is endowed with the power to memorize the road. And what makes a person so humble, if not the mitzvah, which so purifies the flesh as to have it discern the direction of the road. If the power of intuition could reside anywhere at all, it would be where the mitzvah takes it, in the foot, as King David experienced it, when he said, "Your word is a lamp to my feet, and a light to my path."

T he sway that Eastern thinking had on the youth, which had never been as strong as it was in the 1960s, seems to have practically died out. Gone are the days when a white cloak mounted on an emaciated body automatically evidenced that the person under it had surfaced in the world of true bliss. Those were the hungry years. But there is no denying that some of these teachers had something to offer. They had come with a new language, and what they had to say, they said well. Their main objective was to spiritualize the West, and what better means could best further their cause than good old *common sense*, a rare commodity at all times. The plan seemed to have consciously been to first train the mind to think clearly and economically, in other words, prepare the terrain first, before following that with spiritual practice. But things worked better than planned, for no sooner had these teachers begun to loosen tight spirits, than the listeners seemed to reach a nirvanic bliss. People came down for a rest like migrating birds. The teachers took to the clouds from joy. The chemistry was such that any of the teachers' words, whether right or wrong, managed to effect a redemption there. There was no possibility to miss the target. There were targets everywhere. These were ideal times for experimentation. And who could have wished for more fertile ground to redefine intelligence, when Western intelligence was being declared bankrupt? Just consider how little common sense was necessary to convey the type of message the intuitive teachers would spell out. In truth, not much, just enough to give credence to his talks.

You can envision the ripple effect these teachings had on a mind that was so utterly inept at broadening its scope. It was only eager to take a rest. The prevalent expression for such an accommodation was "balance," a state of being that most everyone in this psychologically saturated age still seems to be desperately looking for. What is balance, anyway? Is it an expression of life, its ultimate objective, or a utopian state?

The term used to define the person of Jacob, who harmonized the kindness (*Hesed*) of Abraham and the might (*Gevurah*) of Isaac, is beauty (*Tiferet*), where beauty is an ingenious combination of the two opposite attributes, in a manner such that they do not fuse into one whole, but are kept apart, so that each is given a distinct role to play. In Jacob, attributes alternate with and enhance one another, like the hues of a richly colored fabric. *Might* wears the coat of kingship. *Kindness* dresses in modest garb. And *Beauty* verges toward splendor. There is no mixing of colors. Halftones and quartertones, the grey and beige, issue forth intermittently between the frankly colored surfaces. For it was heavenly decreed, that in Jacob, attributes would essentially be given to express their full potential, this being the perfect manner by which life is sanctified.

As with Jacob, we manifest the opposite attributes that are in all of us. It is a paradox which, if upheld, brings beauty and wisdom into the world. And peace. Not a conceptual peace, one obtained through the contrived harmonizing of opposite forces: affected brotherhood, or some emotive fusion of all creeds, but true peace. The injunction to make manifest the opposite attributes that are in us, to actualize the full spectrum of our true potential, should apply to everyone, with the exception of those in precarious physical or psychological health, in which case "balance" may be an appropriate mode of cure.

For life is not meant to be a long drawn out period of convalescence. If we cannot take risks or conquer new territories, then we cannot actualize our full potential. We ought to present ourselves with the same readiness that we displayed at Sinai, where our response to God's command to accept the Torah, of which we knew nothing, was an unequivocal: "We will do and we will hear!" Our readiness to say yes to the unknown had been our first initiation into the practice of acting without the comfort of equilibrium. For one moment, we had lost our sense of logic, only to find that we had broadened our intelligence. And when we came back to ourselves, we found out how much that momentary lapse of reason had contributed to strengthening the rational mind. Such a shift between the rational and the miraculous has become a familiar exercise by now. This is how the intellect gathers momentum. This is where life is truly lived, and this is where the true man is made. Aside from that, there is either the epicurean, who spends the greatest portion of his existence sampling pleasures, or the philosopher, who does not live life as much as he tries to invest it with meaning. Some epicureans go as far as trying to organize their pursuit of pleasure as a philosophy, and there are people who spend their entire existence somewhere in between. These are the equilibrists, who have more or less control over their desire for the forbidden. They do not make obvious transgressions, but they have one weakness: they indulge in those pleasures that the Law permits. This is precisely what Rabbi Shneur Zalman of Liady, the first Lubavitcher Rebbe, attempts to convey in his book, the *Tanya*, when he cautions against selective love, against a love that is restricted to the immediate members of the family. For while such a love is perfectly legitimate, in the end, it will have a disastrous effect on the family. This love will not endure because it is not nourished by the challenges of the outside world. It will wither in isolation, because it is a love in name only.

The children may be very well behaved, even pious, and quite educated. However, chances are that none of them will leave a noticeable mark on the world. In contrast, when love is given unconditionally, it has a marked influence on the external appearance of its giver. If such a love transfigures the face, will it not, by natural progression, also affect the ambient air?

One evening a visibly troubled young Hasid came to visit. His black wide-brim hat, thick side-curls, and black beard accentuated the intensity in his piercing eyes. He had an angelic face. It took some time before he mentioned, in ambiguous terms, that he had some bouts with depression. All he knew was that he had lost his grip on the reality of life. Very little of it made sense to him. He had not opened a book for months. Even prayer eluded him. He had a bright future ahead of him. He was an *illuy*, a genius, and now he kept himself in seclusion for fear that someone might take notice of his illness. He even dreaded meeting with his close friends, none of whom had seen him since he had returned from Israel, where he had spent the previous two years studying the esoteric texts.

He sat there slumped against the back of his seat, his legs crossed, sizing me up with the insolence of youthful intellect. At first, he reacted to anything I said with either total silence or guarded facial signals. However, it did not take long before he formulated his thoughts after I challenged him to articulate them more clearly. The insolence was still there, but I did not mind it a bit. I liked him very much, just the same. His brilliance forbade him from trusting me completely, or perhaps he chose to keep some distance from me to give more momentum to our talk. Whatever it was, all I know is that he succeeded in having me figure out a more persuasive version of what had caused his trouble. He beamed when I had expected him to exhibit a deadpan reaction to my explanations. I made headway toward helping him, but it was not enough. More discussions would be needed, and describing the nature of his problem was a relatively easy thing for me to do.

Like many others, he had made the fundamental mistake of being too selective in his way of studying the Torah. He had passed over, or paid very little attention to, the legends, the *agadoths* that are narrated between deliberations of laws in the Talmud. He had discarded the "bulk" and taken only the sap, when the bulk, each legend of the Talmud, is the place where preparations are made for a particular law to be resolved. He had acted like those strict vegetarians who, in exclusively consuming mostly essence, hardly eat any "junk" at all, and who, therefore, experience a spiritual burnout. The self-induced depressive state goes unnoticed at first. For the vitality, the biological exhilaration, that is given off by food, temporarily buries well-rooted emotions. And when they do find that they are ill, they might still never realize that their spiritual malaise has actually been caused by an "excess of health." They are *too* clean. Memory has been washed out of the cells in the process. There are no faults, no rough edges, and therefore very little chance for compassionate love.

I explained how a mere story, in an unassuming way, widens the intellect's scope, that it speaks to the whole person, and therefore does not fit the ego. It surprises the mind, the heart, and the kidneys. It gathers all the fragments. I also made sure to tell him how that same mentality of the strict vegetarian, who nourishes himself only with the sap, had prevented him from reaching out to those less fortunate than him. For poor though they may have been, they could have pumped oxygen into his intellect with their vibrant, albeit trivial speech. Consistent with that sort of mentality was the fact that he had no role model, no *Tzaddik* in his life, no hovering light to shelter the essence of his being. The idea about form nourishing the essence apparently pleased him. "Alright," he said, looking at me straight in the eyes, "I agree with almost everything you said. I am only too eager to get a quick recipe for the cure."

I was dumbstruck. Here was someone, who for years had made himself liable to be taken by a force that laid claim on his mind, and who was now asking me to remedy his problem with words. If words were going to suffice, I needed a theater. He pressed me for an answer. I said I needed time. He stood up to leave. I invited him to use our house as a hideout. He politely thanked me for the offer. I emphasized that together, we would find a quick resolution to his crisis, mostly through small talk during meals. He thanked me again, but by then, I realized that he did not believe me capable of helping him. Or perhaps he thought that I could, but probably found it demeaning that I chose to help his distinguished person with such simplistic means.

I reiterated my offer as he was getting up to leave, but his eyes were already saying, "Thanks, not for me."

For days I felt remorseful. Why hadn't I tried to help him on his own terms? I consoled myself with having given him an accurate diagnosis. At least, he had that to work with. There remained the possibility that he would come down willy nilly to the same resolution that I offered. But how capable was he to actualize it on his own? Who would have the foresight, the patience, the readiness of spirit, to exchange wisdom for an action that is especially designated to pull him out of his void? Who knows? Perhaps his recovery was at hand.

The thought that this segment of history, called by our sages the "Heels of the Redeemer," is in its final phase, lends validity to my wish that the Hasid's feet find their way. It remains to be known what would be the nature of the action that could bring his ailing mind to safety. Which deed is more suitable to effect the cure?

The deed is a horse and thought is its rider. The rider is a warrior king who plunges into the thick of the battle. The communication between the two is ideal. One day, the king is wounded, and his fighting arm is made heavy. So severe is his wound that his weakened body has to lean on the mount, who, in sensing the difference, understands that it must take command. Quickly it disengages itself from the melee to gallop back to its stall.

11

T HE GENERATIVE principle, known as the attribute of *Yesod* (Foundation), is also called "All" by the Kabbalists. In the human realm, this "All" is the *Tzaddik*, the Just, for all that exists, as it is said, is made from him, who is the substance of the world. It is with him in mind that the Creator brought forth all of Creation. He is the teacher whose body is as refined as our souls. He frees us from our private Egypts. He is the king-poet whose prayer is composed with the innermost song of every human heart. He is the redeemer, whose heels are the voice of this last generation, and whose name of consolation was hidden since the first Saturday night of the world.

And all words speak of him . . . .

THE NIGHT OF THE JUST

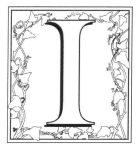T IS A PREVALENT custom among observant Jews to gather on Saturday night, to sing and dance and tell stories until dawn. We extend the *Shabbat* that has technically passed, to carry some of its holiness with us into the profane. It is the ideal time to speak about the Just. Any story or anecdote about them is a Shabbat in itself, a rest stop for the Jew who is preparing to confront the weekdays. It is a place of transition where the mind is given ample time to ready itself for the mundane.

The *other side* has been starving during the entire length of Shabbat. Therefore, you can only expect that as soon as Shabbat draws to its end, the *other side* will reach out to devour the defenseless. It lies in wait by the doors of every house of prayer and grabs congregants by the dozen. One bite from the beast, and they are infused with an acute sense of the Saturday night blues.

For those who keep watch, Saturday night is a most sacred time, when exile is boxed in by redemption. It is a time when the nourishment of the spirit is most varied, when all duality is resolved.

Intelligence is acute; everyone who celebrates the occasion is instantly wise. Doubts wane. Impossible questions are easily answered. The night exhausts itself, depositing a block of resolutions.

It is the night when the true face of the Jew emerges. The subtle mixture of light and darkness gives a brightly hued, vibrant luminosity to the ambient air in which the face reveals ancient wisdom. The image is somewhat grainy, because neither light nor darkness is yet settled in its respective vessel. But in their eager jockeying for position, in that play of volatile contrasts, the true face is exposed.

Shabbat bathes the Jew in a bright and homogenous light which is not necessarily conducive to revelations of individual character. Shabbat is much too full, and therefore permits no contrast. Shabbat is the reservoir, not the conduit. It is contained within specific limits which allow no explosions to occur. Saturday night's light, however, flickers relentlessly. It is a black fire whose pulsating luminescence disturbs and disperses the obtrusive layers that camouflage the soul. The Jew is never more conscious of his mission than during these hours. It is on this night that the world was created and on the very same night that light was made. Now, light is again renewed through our actions. As Shabbat draws to its end, and the obscurity of night begins to cover us with its black mantle, we burn a braided candle, whose variegated and animated flame rekindles the light of creation.

Our holy masters say that the feeling of sadness we experience at Shabbat's end is caused by our subconscious sense of the primordial Breaking of the Vessels—that timeless, spaceless juncture in the history of creation when the divine light fell into the lower worlds. We are given a taste of that decline. The light of Shabbat has flown back to its nest, and we search for it within. Some mystical writings compare that departure of the light to a deer fleeing from its pursuer, running with its head tilted under and to the side, staring back into our eyes. In that look of the deer, as the light recedes swiftly in the distance, we are given to retroactively appreciate the hidden reality of Shabbat.

The same applies to *Tzaddikim*, who are so holy that they must literally withdraw to a distance in order to transmit their message. In nearness, one glimpses only a token of their luminescence. But at the moment of separation, one last look from them hits us with a radiance which fills us to the brim. One could be shattered in that awesome moment. The best advice is to take the light and run. You are never sure whether it is a look of severity or of love, perhaps a love so pure and strong, it must borrow some severity in order to arrive. Whichever it may be, that singular expression in the eyes of the *Tzaddik* provides one with an abundance of nourishment that grows in tandem with a deepening strictness of spirit, which inspires one to keep in line.

The physical presence of the *Tzaddikim* is so exceedingly precious, that it could touch those who are able to appreciate them with tinges of sadness, even at the moment when joy is at its peak. We have just met the *Tzaddik*, and already cannot bear to leave him. We are overcome with a sense that this is too good to be real. Yet here, the sadness is of the positive kind, serving to quicken the joy with which it intertwines. It may just be that Jewish intelligence acquires some of its keenness and profundity in the subtle interplay between sadness and joy. Bitterness, in small, homeopathic dosages, expands the limits of understanding. The solemn look that the deer throws back at us from a distance tones our spirit. It is an invitation to transcend every profane thought which may come our way during the week. Two rays shoot forth from the deer's eyes. Each is a protection against an unforeseeable fall, like rails on either side of a windy bridge.

It is said that at the beginning of Creation, on Saturday night, the vessels broke. On that same night, the repair of the vessels also began. From this tradition, I can only assume that there is no more opportune time to repair our own. Darkness was formed when work was left undone. The mundane week lies before us like an open abyss, auguring a reprise of that tragedy. The abyss beckons, and its pull is far out of proportion to our fragilities. This disparity is the main cause of Saturday night melancholia. The threat is real.

So real in fact, that one cannot possibly remain insensitive to it, since all of us descend from Adam, who was the first to experience the fall. It is said that upon seeing the sun set for the first time, he experienced great anguish, certain that darkness had settled on the world because of his sin. That very same night, he took two stones and struck them one against the other until sparks flew. Though such a simple act seemed to hold little promise of transcendence, it was, in fact, the initial stroke that impelled him to return to the Garden of Eden. Poor though it may have been, the light of the fire gave him comfort, and so he blessed it. The memory of that past makes of Saturday night a most opportune time for new beginnings. Anticipation of something new happening is never so great, which is the reason why this night is known as the "Night of the Redeemer."

According to tradition, the Redeemer will reveal himself in the blink of an eye, even when all the signs and estimations will concur to proclaim his coming. He will surprise everyone, wicked or wise, and also the cautious, those who prefer not to speak about him, for fear of exacerbating others' skepticism, or from taking the risk of spoiling the suspense of his coming. Above all, he will most likely surprise those who think and speak of him constantly, even those who serve him. In accordance with this, we are left with no other alternative than to opt for the obvious. The Redeemer will surprise primarily those who expect him the most, as a mother is surprised by the presence of her child, the same with couples, or true friends, for the simple reason that true surprise hits more strongly those who have much life in them. Others, who have less, will most likely find it hard to react enthusiastically to the news.

It is precisely in such an atmosphere of anticipation, namely, that we could at any moment be taken unawares by something already known, that past faults can be corrected. If folly so treacherously intrudes inside us, to have us commit an error, it is perfectly sensible, therefore, to utilize such means which would take the intruder by surprise. What better scheme is there than to confront the faults during moments that seem so uncertain as to confound them? Being that a fault is, on the whole, of an accidental nature, it is logical that it be exposed to an atmosphere that suits its character. Saturday night's incomplete light makes it an ideal host. No judgment is passed.

But take heed. Don't be so readily fooled by such a display of leniency. The diminished light does not indicate some sort of deficiency or weakness. In truth, the reason why light has dimmed is because it has traveled a distance to gather momentum, before coming back with a force that renews creation. Kabbalah calls such a light "*Or Hozer,*" the

Returning Light. It comes to wake us up from sleep. It says, "Where were you while I was there in your midst? I was a willing guest and you were such a distracted host." It is Shabbat speaking. Distance makes it talk. It has divested itself of its clothing of effervescent gold, and donned a humbler robe to travel lightly.

As the night advances, our faults change aspects. The deeds that are performed for selfish gain are released from bondage. There is no visible trace of corruption in any of them. This occurs because the night makes us more compassionate to ourselves. Or else it is making us wise that we can discern some of the workings of redemption. In any event, the fact is that at such times faults greatly contribute to enriching the atmosphere, while the night kindly obliges by returning the favor with a gift all its own. It broadens the scope of each fault as far as the twilight of Creation. There the fault becomes deed, the instant it re-enters its original mold. You can imagine how much such a moment of goodwill can benefit anyone, stranger or friend. What appears to him most improbable will resolve itself in the warmth of companionship. His faults experience a loss of identity. They have become new entities altogether. They are enriching reality. The interaction between each fault and the specific hour of the night, formulates the mode of the celebration at hand. The mysterious manner with which those wondrous modulations take place, changes between one reality to another, one entity to another, is strongly suggestive of the phenomenon of biological transmutations, a fairly new scientific discovery, which has come to explain how, with a relatively small amount of energy, some type of pressure, a catalyst, and a certain duration of time, some elements can, through the release of one proton, turn into an entirely different element in the process. The exchange is as vital to the giver as it is to the receiver. In other words, it is not a surplus proton, but an integral part of the element that is being given away. Perhaps, in the giving of such a vital part of itself, the element might perish, or perhaps it will gain a new life through such a loss. The stakes are high. The element takes a risk, nevertheless. It takes a leap of faith; it offers itself as a sacrifice, thereby ensuring that life is upheld. And so, reality pulsates through such a critical moment of change, from matter to non matter, existence and nonexistence.

On Saturday night, it is quite visible that the guests experience change the moment they enter the house. However, no transmutation will really begin to take place before the food is served. The animation of the voices generates enough warmth to fecundate the most sterile of thought. The multitude of bodies produces more than enough pressure to wring out bothersome ruminations. The heart is jolted by Hasidic chants. Music, which usually follows, tears all worries apart. But nothing appears more catalyzing than dance, when every remnant of pain, that of dancer and onlookers alike, is shaken off with each change of cadence. The highlight of the celebration, however, will take place in the calm before dawn, when most people have left. By then everyone is weary. Words are few and the movements slow. Silence prevails in spite of the resonance of voices or the fracas of pots being washed. Not even the dissonant chords played by dilettante musicians are able to disrupt the quiescence of the moment. At this stage, incidental noises are put at the service of silence to give it a new depth. Thus nested, thought is given to witness how the passing of time has fulfilled the night's promises—the cycle of transmutations is virtually completed—and subsequently, the slowest metabolism has benefitted as well. At any moment, all this abundance of human exchange ignites time, which shoots back far into the past, to redeem it. The past, in turn, redeems the present. Creation has just begun.

I magine that someone who needs to rest his mind comes to visit. His pain makes him so sensitive, he has hardly passed the door, yet he can already tell how good the hosts are. He knows from the architecture that the house was not built for him, only for the family. He is jolted by the walls and feels insulted by the arrangement of the furniture. He walks sideways, one shoulder forward, one trailing behind, desperately attempting to break his way through reluctant air pressure. He can hear your silent walls telling him that the house has not accepted many guests in the recent past.

You ought to know that most guests come to houses to shed their faults. They assume that your house is a good place for that. You ought to be aware that their faults are besieging their minds, talking nonsense to them. So say nothing when they enter. Let the walls make the presentations. Let the walls answer their questions.

And if you absolutely must speak, be sparing with words. Don't count solely on your mouth to solve people's problems. You may need to say nothing more than, "Please come to the table" or "Did you have a good night's sleep?" They will let you know if you have to add anything. Do not take advantage of them just because they are on your home ground. Ask not whether they have eaten; just serve them food. Do not give weight to your favors, and refrain from inquiring as to the object of their visit. Act as if there is none, and do not try to pull their little secrets out of them.

Do not ask what they do for a living. But above all, do not attempt to figure out their faults with imprudent inquiries, for this will only serve to degrade the quality of companionship. You should aim, instead, at upgrading their vision of reality, which boils down to seeing their faults as inclinations, rather than as terminal afflictions. Their faults are momentary deportations which seem to be caused by overexposure to exile, which is to say that they are not necessarily self inflicted. Some of them could have been acquired at birth. Others enter all of us without permission, like hordes of invisible insects which pile up refuse that thickens and hardens until it causes a change in the personality. These sclerotic deposits have a Hebrew name: *yesh*. It is usually translated as materiality or grossness, and is the determinant of a person's ego. The dregs keep collecting even as the face remains composed. It makes one person secretly hateful and another a liar. It makes one become more arrogant with age, while someone else turns into a thief, an atheist, an idol worshipper or worse, a hypocrite. It boils down to saying that faults are pivotal forces, inasmuch as they contribute to making us singular and unique. They defeat us, but they also build us, as is witnessed in the case of writers who are paradoxically as indebted to a creeping deficiency as to any human qualities. Their genius often derives from their inability to punctuate a sentence. Their thoughts veer and ramble, forcing them to improvise marathon phrases that throb with life.

A fault, whether we want it or not, has a vulgarity which pleases. It is not uncommon that we find ourselves loving people all the more when they would be more fit to be despised. As is evidenced by the confabulations of liars who absorb our attention with their lies, we are charmed because there is so much life in their superlative descriptions. Upon careful scrutiny, however, we will find that they may actually be trying to express truth, when its official spokesmen are, for some reason, unable to spell it out. One can look at it as pure survival instinct on their part, to consume truth in any way it is produced. One may also assume that their strange relation with truth is caused simply by a lack of education. They have never been formally introduced to truth, so they invent it. They stage it and play it with abandon, hoping to capture it as actors do.

Therefore, utmost caution is mandatory in one's dealings with other people's faults, as any attempt to correct them, subtle though it may be, will only serve to add so much more complexity to the problem at hand as to thwart any chance of recovery. Sometimes the evidence is so real that there is more *joie de vivre* in the faults, and we are left with no other choice than to urge those who suffer them to keep them like an endogenous growth which cannot be cut off lest the person bleed to death, or until, by all manner of means, a more conclusive mode of treatment is found.

Until that happens, our homes can offer some respite to the tormented mind. They could fill the role of those "cities of refuge" which existed in Israel in biblical times, where offenders, who had committed unintentional crimes such as manslaughter, would run for shelter. We would entertain them, amuse them, make all sorts of diversions to stave off the ominous attack of the past. We would organize Saturday nights just for them. And we would dance. For how can one rid oneself of a thousand faults if not through dance? I am speaking of Hasidic dance, naturally, when faults are made so confused that they lose contact with their past, becoming different entities altogether. They so enjoy their new character that they want to dance all night. What makes such moments all the more exciting, however, is the fact that the dancer is completely lost in the crowd. The last thing he wants at this point is attention. He would rather make it on his own. He screams as he dances, to expel every begrudging thought. As he is pushed to the center of the floor, the other dancers have unknowingly established a space within which his redemption begins to take form. It won't be long before he senses a fullness welling up within himself, which can only mean that the Saturday night light has finally found its abode.

You knock at heaven's door, and give your name. They say they never heard of you. You have been gone for so long you are not on their list, but the King remembers you. He had sent you on a mission, but you got lost in the abyss. The King says, "Make room for this man. He is bringing news." The entire court, all of them noble souls, makes way to form a corridor as you walk, breathless, toward the throne. You bless the King's Name with each step. You proclaim that everything written in the sacred books is true; that He is true and His Torah is true and the man Moses is true. You saw it with your own eyes down there in the recesses of the world. They bring out maps, the charts of Creation, to verify whether your journey corresponds to Heaven's design, whether you have fulfilled the King's dearest wish: to build a small dwelling for Him in the lower depths of the world.

You feel great shame, seeing the holy members of the court making way for you. You stand there apologizing for your poor person, for your past, with repetitious and ostensible bows, even as they urge you to proceed.

Some of them cannot resist asking questions. "How was it down there in the abyss?" They want to know. They are eager to hear how you staged your return, to which you gladly oblige by explaining that rather than reaching up for the Divine, you went further down instead, digging wells, only to find that the waters down there have the same blueness of which the heavens are made. You explain how, in spite of the fact that at some point you knew your way out, you chose to dwell in the depths, digging, while nevertheless anticipating the thrill of meeting with the King. You go on describing how, in your mind, you figured out that perhaps in digging deep below the very place where you stand, you extended the distance between the heavens and the earth. You established an outpost, thus promoting a vigorous circulation between the heavens and the new frontier. This had been your main preoccupation but you are not so certain that it was effective. "Indeed it was," one of the members of the court admits. "Nothing moves Heaven more than when one locates a new limit," he continues. "Originally," adds another member of the court, "the limit in question has, since Creation, been the established distance, only it was not explored. Now, it is you who are blazing the trail. You have made God known in the depths!"

You have earned the title "Master of Return," for you left none of your belongings in the abyss. You did not commit the dreadful error to rid yourself of your past, as one does an old cloth. Instead of discarding your faults indiscriminately, you first attempted to make them into assets, either by recycling them or replacing them in the correct context. You went as far as using what was decidedly evil in some of them as fuel for your return trip, which amounts to saying that you have succeeded in turning every one of your mistakes into merits.

You thank everyone and kiss every hand as you pass. "If not for your help," you shout at the top of your lungs, "I would still be there in the abyss! Thank God, Who has created the Just. Thank God, Who has put in my passage a true *Tzaddik*, a warrior king, who deserves the title "Master of Return," insofar as he has redeemed my past and the past of Israel. For my *Tzaddik*, my Rebbe, my redeemer, fulfills a dual role, that of *Shabbat*, the settled light, and of *Or Hozer*, the returning light. For years, his light kept coming at me to purify my flesh, so as to make it a more fitting vessel."

"I have toiled with my own hands, it is true, but how does that compare with the effect of just one of his blessings? When, for instance, my instinct in the past had been to use force to make my point, either through speech or political stratagem, he blessed me with pleasant conduct. From that day on, I made it my business to keep my mouth shut, to ascertain that my words would not cause irreparable damage. I learned that an answer, true though it may be, rather than resolving a conflict, would only serve to fan the fire. At times it seemed as though I was holding a wild animal by the leash. I remained mute. By then, however, either my old opponent had picked the answer out of the air or he had probably grown wise enough to figure it out on his own.

Nothing pleased me more than that. For is there anything more pleasant to the soul than helping someone to grow independent? In that sense, because I have tamed the animal in me, in so far as to have the animal respect my wish to make peace with the adversary, I may have deserved, in my own modest way, the all too honorable title of 'Master of Return.'"

It happened some years ago. The *Tzaddik*, man of God, Lamp of Israel, Head of the Kabbalists, Rabbi Mordechai Sharabi, may his memory be blessed, had just passed away in Jerusalem. We were all deeply grieved. That same week, right after Shabbat, we were notified of the imminent visit to our house of a kabbalist, recently arrived from Israel. The news cheered us a bit. We decided with friends who had shared Shabbat with us, that it was Divine Providence that such a person would come into our lives at such a precise time. We could not wait for the moment when he would share with us some wise words. When he came in, followed by a few young men, he looked impressive. He was about sixty years old, very tall and thin, and bent over. His long earlocks swung back and forth, giving one the impression that they propelled his walk, as if he was in flight. The house suddenly became silent to welcome all that majesty. Everyone seemed to avert his eyes when we sat around the dining room table. He intimidated all of us. Nevertheless I found enough courage to look straight into his feverish black eyes, but he glanced elsewhere.

As it turned out, a friend who had served for a while as an assistant to Rabbi Sharabi, sat beside me. He took advantage of the moment when the visitor had his head turned to murmur his praise in my ear. The man was purported to be an exceptional teacher of Kabbalah. The object of his visit, I was informed, was to collect money for his *yeshiva*. I was asked if I could participate in the fundraising by introducing our visitor to some willing donors. My friend invited me to extend such an offer, or at least give some words of encouragement, but I remained mute. Not that I was unwilling to oblige, I sensed that something was awry. The visitor did not strike me as being a kabbalist of pure intent, in the sense that he had not nullified his person to the extent of making himself a vessel fit to receive the esoteric. However, I would not go as far as putting him in the same category as those New Age kabbalists whose contact with the esoteric is confined to paraphrased English editions solemnly taught in bourgeois settings. This is Kabbalah for the beginner, for the tourist in metaphysics, an esotericism for the hard core romantic, if not some type of release therapy for the guilty conscience.

By contrast, our visitor, as I understood, had a reputation of being well versed in both the esoteric and exoteric scripture. It is quite probable that his eyes had read more pages of books than they had seen people, and that his mouth had spoken more of sacred subjects than of mundane topics. At least he had something real to offer. But try as I might, I just could not help being uncomfortable in his presence. I could not put a finger on what it was that caused that feeling in me, until I discovered something unsettling about his mouth, more precisely, in his upper lip. It looked as though it had been abused by occasional contortions of disgust, and kabbalists, I gathered, would certainly not make any such grimace, which I anticipated he would execute any moment. For several minutes, there was hardly an exchange of words. The silence thickened to the point of becoming intolerable. Doubt was eating me up. What if I was wrong in my judgment? I had an idea. I would have my friend ask the visitor whether he knew that Rabbi Sharabi had passed away, and whether he had known Rabbi Sharabi or had studied with him.

Now you should know, from the first, that no one in his right mind would have dared gain entry in esoteric study, and the teaching of it, without the consent and blessing of Rabbi Sharabi. He was the gate to that world. He was known for having achieved the mind-boggling feat of completing the entire Talmud by the age of eight. For some reason, he had not opened a book during the last thirty years of his life. He enjoyed having his disciples take turns reading for him, and while they did he would quote, with a staggering precision, entire paragraphs, either from the book itself or from related sources. He remembered everything he had learned. If he made a quote, he would indicate its exact location—the book, the page, even the line, sometimes mentioning on which shelf, and how many books from the right or the left, that particular book stood.

I heard from various sources how some privileged disciples, upon entering his room, had seen him shine with blinding light by the hour of midnight; whereas most of those who visited him attest to having caught the smell of the *etrog* fruit around his person. For all that, the fact is that none of those who had known him, or had only heard of him, would deny that the mere mention of his name purified the already pristine air of Jerusalem.

Therefore, what the visitor ought to have done, upon hearing Rabbi Sharabi's name mentioned, was to lower his head and be shaken to his toes. But he did not. His upper lip curled up instead, just as I had anticipated that it would. He followed that with an impassionate "Yes, we have met." That's all he said. I assume that everyone present understood what such a dull reaction meant: "I am not so small myself." I felt nauseated. I have only vague recollections of how that meeting ended. What I recall, however, is that it did not last long, and that the visitor left empty-handed.

Weeks, or perhaps months, went by before the explanation for my previous predisposition of having anticipated the visitor's grimace, came to mind one day. I discovered that such a predisposition was not so much an inborn talent as it was an acute sense of appreciation for the real that I had developed during my sojourn in the abyss. During my exile, light proved insistently superior to darkness, so that when I eventually surfaced onto the promised ground, the real stood distinctly apart from the false. I found myself assessing situations through contrasts. Instead of reflecting upon making a choice with as keen an intellect as would be normally required, I would do nothing more than project an image of the real as I had experienced it—whether it was an indescribable moment of the past, or a face, or the name of a *Tzaddik*—against whatever situation I was confronted with, to obtain the most startling revelations. The opposing of one type of reality against another did away with crippling uncertainties. I was made immune to the habit of asking too many questions. The readings of situations were as quick as they were impartial. Essence revealed itself easily through form. I could, in one quick gaze, tell how much sacredness simmered behind even the most stoic of faces. One quick gaze was enough to measure the extent of the heart's influence on the intellect, and vice versa. And if it happened that the person I faced was a scholar, to what degree, and to what end, for good or for evil, had his learning affected his actions? Was the attachment between his thoughts and his deeds so real and so solid as to form a bridge that I could cross without apprehension?

To conclude, it has been said that the most insignificant gestures of the *Tzaddik* are dearer to God than his scholarly achievements. If such is the truth, it could possibly justify one in supposing that the hosts of heaven are as taken up by those gestures as well. It would not be that much more unreasonable to assume how the attention given to mere physical movements may turn out to be one of their favorite pastimes. And if such is the case, one can easily imagine their dismay when seeing the *Tzaddik* conform to the trivial exigencies of existence, such as, for instance, adjusting his hat, blowing his nose, or stroking his beard. This seems to imply that since they are all too aware of the exceptional degree of spirituality of the *Tzaddik*, angels ought to be as equally shocked by the materialization of his movements as we are understandably shocked by the materialization of thought in the physical brain. Every one of those movements is as novel and as spiritually revealing to them as a newly created thought is to intelligence. The degree of completion of the *Tzaddik* is such that his physical appearance must be an overt expression of his essence. It deeply affects us. In this instance, Heaven wants the power of thought or speech to be upstaged by something as unassuming as the form. If the world, as it is said, stands on the actions of the *Tzaddik,* then the world must adjust itself to the grace with which those casual gestures are executed. We sway like reeds in the breeze each time he simply shifts his body, lifts his hand, breaks bread, or brings a cup full of wine to his lips. And when we leave his presence to go into the world, we cannot help but discern falsehood, however concealed it may be. Our senses are so offended by the dichotomy. We can tell by the way someone walks whether he is walking with life, or against it. And if we are truly responsive to impure or unjust action, we are able to perceive how the light of the *Tzaddik* has cast shadows on the face of the usurper.

O ur happiest celebrations in Morocco took place in Jewish cemeteries. People would lock their houses, close shop, squeeze themselves into buses, or in the back of trucks, together with bedding and foodstuffs, to go celebrate the anniversary of a *Tzaddik's* passing at his burial ground. For days, if not weeks, we camped in tents. Adults would pray, recite Psalms and read the *Zohar*. Children played all sorts of games among the graves. When night came, everyone, great and small, scholars and simple folk, gathered around the storytellers. No one thought himself in any way superior to his neighbor. The spirit of generosity prevailed. Lamb was roasted in the open. Families competed for guests. Beggars were spoiled with gifts. Money constantly changed hands. Candles were lit by the pack. *Mahia*, our traditional alcoholic drink, flowed like water.

The unity among us could not have been more ideal. If the beauty of sight and spirit of the camp at the foot of Sinai cannot be equaled, our own camp, with our Arabic tents and great multitude, was closest to resembling it. In any event, those were the scenes on which we were weaned. I am tempted to say that it was in those holy places that much of our enduring fear of Heaven was obtained. The same is true for our uncomplicated faith in God, as well as for our openness of mind to the reality of *Tzaddikim*, and our flair for recognizing them, whether they be hidden or revealed. We grew to trust them. We do not know what it is like to doubt them, the immediate compensation being that it affects us deeply enough to render us immune to morbid suspicions of other people's existence. Our nature is to believe that everyone we meet is more righteous than we are. We have nothing in us that would spontaneously create enemies. Kind faces enchant us. We are naive because it is less problematic. That is better than having to constantly be on the lookout, a disposition that unfailingly leads to narrow-mindedness and intolerance, or perhaps to having such a divisive spirit that it splits the people of Israel apart.

It is therefore not surprising that in our tradition a cemetery is called "The House of the Living." It is quite evident that life is nowhere more emphatically stated than on those grounds, if only for the simple reason that they compel one to reflect on the preciousness of existence. Also, it could very well be that out of gratitude for paying homage to the dead, God consents to extend the length of our days. The Kabbalistic texts teach that visiting the resting place of Tzaddikim causes new intelligences to descend upon the world. Prayers rise. It is no wonder then that the air in the proximity of those places makes one wise. That being the case, imagine the positive effect those places have on a soul that has lost all sense of direction, or for that matter, how much more responsive the bearer of that soul would become to the certainty of redemption. Therefore, we should not find it surprising that pilgrims invariably concur in their reports that those places in the Diaspora have very much the same atmosphere as that of the Land of Israel.

W hen the righteous man of God and light of the world, Rabbi Israel Abehsera, a distant relative, passed away some years ago in Israel, five hundred thousand people participated in the procession that took him to his place of rest. They all had come to pay respect to the man who had cried and prayed for them, who had served them food and drink with his own hands, had toasted them with glasses of *mahia*, and had sung along with them, even until the very last day of his life. He was a scholar of the highest order, in both the revealed and hidden Torah. He knew the Talmud by heart. He was Kabbalah personified; yet, he taught none of that, not in a traditional manner anyway. His way was to translate his vast knowledge into action by attending to people's needs. Rabbis came for advice, childless couples to be blessed for children, and the sick to be healed. He led the same type of life as that of Rabbi Israel Baal Shem Tov, after whom he was named. Arabs in Morocco often saw him studying in the midst of lions in the Atlas Mountains. His achievements knew no limit. He was blessed with the highest nobility of spirit, and yet he would often insist on being blessed by people who were not heedful of the Law. Simply because he loved them with a love so pure, he might have judged it ludicrous to change their ways on the spot. He limited his role to that of making room for them, leaving it to God to do the rest. Miracles fell like rain.

I was relating some of those miracles to a visitor when he informed me of some disparaging remarks a rabbi had made about the people who, as he put it, find nothing better to do with their lives than visiting the graves of *Tzaddikim*. The rabbi singled out the Breslover Hasidim, who travel annually to Uman, in the Ukraine, to pray at the grave of Rabbi Nachman, their Rebbe, and added shifty comments and insinuations about the miracles of Rabbi Israel Abehsera, letting it be understood, without really saying it, how they might not have been in line with Jewish Law.

I was furious. My indignation grew even more intense when my guest admitted, after I inquired, that he had done nothing to counter the rabbi's venomous comments. He had never been any good himself at engaging in debate, least of all with a rabbi who was twice his age. He recognized that by remaining silent, he had, in effect, given his tacit consent to those comments. At first, I was not going to subject him to any manner of reproof. He was much too delicate for that, but my frustration was such that I felt compelled to condemn the guilty rabbi. I launched a denunciation of him which lasted for quite some time. I declared that he should be stripped of the title which he had dishonored, and that, if it were up to me, I would pull off his hat, which he no longer deserved, and top his head with a dunce's cap instead, as punishment for having slandered two *Tzaddikim* with his corrupting breath.

For days after that, I ruminated on ways to refute the rabbi's thoughtless comments, at the same time being too mindful that a meeting between us was very unlikely. For who wants to be the mouthpiece of a cause that is rooted in hot air? Who would want to make public his doubt in God's ability to create someone so pure that he cannot possibly commit a transgression? Therefore, it is only fair to suppose that, in taking the law into his own hands, the rabbi got so emotionally involved in holding on tight to the law which he championed, that he truncated his vision of the world. I could only picture him as a child whose dreams about becoming a policeman were realized in religion. He clears traffic. He cannot read faces. He cannot tell the difference between a street "wonder worker" whose skill is the consequence of his spiritual deficiency, and a *Tzaddik* who delivers his miracles from an overflow of excellence. He cannot tell that the miracles of the *Tzaddik* are the natural consequence of his person, the sparks of his fire, that they are a manna which comes in all forms and flavors; that they are small material down payments, every one of them stamped and approved by Heaven, which come down through some prodigious process of transmutation, through the merit of the *Tzaddik's* vast wisdom. Therefore the miracles will not subject anyone to servitude, since wisdom is always fair.

M any years ago, I received a visit from the man who wanted me to arrange a meeting for him with the Lubavitcher Rebbe. He had come all the way from London. He had called me minutes before boarding the plane to inform me of his imminent visit, even after I made a few attempts to discourage him from coming. We had hardly sat down when he said, quite agitated, that he had an important question that only the Rebbe could answer. But when I explained that it would be impossible to obtain an audience, especially on such short notice, he took it very badly. At some point, he got up and started pacing the floor, repeating many times as he paced that he would surely die if his question was not answered immediately. To quiet him down, I promised to try to obtain the audience in a month, but that only served to accelerate his pacing. He was getting on my nerves. I got up and stopped him. "Look," I said while locking him with my two arms, "What's your question? I'll answer it." His eyes widened. "Who do you think you are?" he said, but that did not discourage me in the least. I repeated my offer. This time around, however, he pulled away from me with such violence that it was lucky that I did not fall. I pursued him, while he begged me to keep away. My feeling was that his question was not as crucial as he thought. It was not even a question, but rather a noise, which may have been caused somewhere in his psyche, which stood in the form of a big question mark. I believed that once all that excess was dissolved, his question would automatically dissolve with it. All he needed for that to happen was good company. I attempted to tell him that, but he would not listen. Instead, he threatened to go knock at the Rebbe's door, and he was not bluffing. He had me trapped. To show good faith, I phoned the Rebbe's secretary, who apologetically explained that there were hundreds of people on the waiting list, which meant weeks of waiting, and therefore my visitor would do well to put his question in writing. When he heard that, he flew into a rage and spoke of his imminent death as he reached for his coat.

I threw myself across the doorway to block his path, pleading with him to confide in me, but he pushed me away. "I'm really sorry to tell you that you're no match for what's on my mind," he said sardonically, after which he begged that I move out of his way. But I did not budge. "What is so great and so new about your question that I can't answer it?" I asked while restraining him. "All questions have already been asked," I continued. "Most of them are known. It is only your impatience that makes yours look so unique. So ask it, will you?" I demanded. Again he pushed me and proceeded to the exit door. "You should be forgiven for this," he said in an affected tone of voice, as he reached for the doorknob. I was going to lose him. He was going to leave with the wrong idea. I felt a terrible guilt for confusing him. I had to find a remedy for that. "You know what," I said while searching for words, "think what you want—hate me, judge me, but I must tell you this. Ask that question of yours, will you, and I will give you a *better* answer than the Rebbe!" His eyes bulged out of their sockets. My head grew hot and my pulse raced. I felt faint. "I'm going to report you. I'm going to tell the whole world what you said," he concluded with disgust. He turned and began to walk away, but I would not give up so easily. I knew what to do. I was going to tell him that although my reaction didn't seem to make sense to the intellect, and it appeared mad by all manners of criteria, I had to say it that way, because if he gave me time, I could perhaps succeed in explaining that his answer, and for that matter any answer, even the final answer to redemption, resides in the *small*, meaning *us*, the people; with the stipulation, however, that we go beyond our doubts and means, shooting ahead of intellect, being unmindful as to whether intellect gives us permission to proceed or not. I also wanted to explain how that momentary lapse of reason that one experiences is the surest antidote to vanity; how it happens so quickly that the ego is not given a chance to gorge itself on one extra breath of air. Another reason that vanity has no part in any of this is that there is no planning involved whatsoever, that the mind cannot contain the thought which instigates that sort of action.

I prepared myself to also tell him that I would readily mire my lips in mud and forbid myself to let any more words come out of my mouth, rather than mean what I had said in the rather simplistic way that he had chosen to hear it. I would really choose to rot between worms before it happens that I, the idiot of the Rebbe, his buffoon, a thickhead, would begin to formulate the thought of surpassing even a speck of the wisdom of the man who made me.

I caught up with him at the bottom of the stairs and entreated him to listen to what I had to say. Luckily, he agreed. However, he did it so ungracefully. He planted himself before me with his arms crossed, so that it made me lose momentum. My words tripped over my tongue, and when I finally managed to make sense, he stood as defiant as ever, with a hand behind his ear, to signal that he had difficulty understanding me.

I tried as best I could not to let myself be intimidated by his stance as I spoke rather expediently about how *Tzaddikim* are under constant surveillance, how there is a specific clause in their contract with Heaven which stipulates that they cannot give one answer too many, how the *other side* stands ready to make sure that the combat is fair. "Redemption must come from the people," the other side keeps on clamoring. Therefore, I did nothing other than follow the will of Heaven when I spoke the way I did. And that was precisely the Rebbe's wish, as it is the wish of all true *Tzaddikim*, that we conquer new territories with our small means, that we be so free, so utterly unaware of our limitations as to crack open practical little secrets the *Tzaddikim* are not allowed to reveal. "And now," I said to my visitor, who was still caught in his defiant pose, "will you ask your question please?" Instead he laughed as he searched for his car keys. "I'm sorry," he said as he walked away, "but there is something that is definitely warped with you Hasidim."

T he event that I am about to relate has already been mentioned, albeit briefly, in an earlier chapter. It is an event that has grown to the dimension of a Hasidic tale, to say nothing of the fact that this one especially typifies the inordinate manner with which Hasidic intelligence at certain times expresses itself. In that sense, it is fit to be told on Saturday night, when truth comes dressed with extravagance, for the distinct purpose of defusing the eruptive waves of Saturday night blues.

It is about whistling, a sound which I suppose every Jewish parent, from one generation to the next, warned his children against doing, impressing the mind with the idea that it was so evil that it summoned demons. It was the sound of flutes, my father would tell us, that helped to destroy the Holy Temple. But now, the Rebbe has come to the rescue of that sound. He has redeemed it from the enemy's arsenal of war, and restored it to a more noble function.

Even after the whistling had been going on for years, we were unable to come up with a rationale for the Rebbe's command, though there was no lack of speculation. I suspect that many Hasidim have shared my first perception of it as being that we are all blowing our own *shofar*. Over the years, I have also, among other explanations, come to think of it as a particularly effective way to clamor for Heaven's attention. If we were to try to be as effective with our voices, we would soon destroy our throats. Although it does have its role, the voice can only carry so far. A good song can be as eloquent as prayer, but when darkness hangs over us like ominous clouds, song humbly plays second fiddle to the whistle. The reason behind the ability of the whistle to shatter those clouds lies in the fact that every fiber of the being gets involved in the combat. Even thought is determined to break its abstractness into breath. All parts convene to form a united front.

On the more pragmatic side, as far as my immediate experience is concerned, the whistling, when it happens, presents me with the rare opportunity to make full use of my lungs, for I find it difficult to breathe easily outside of Jerusalem. Jews, in general, are not too keen on exercise. Physical feats are mostly Greek to us, although we do need to take a deep breath once in a while to keep a check on existence.

About a year after we started whistling, during a gathering around the Rebbe, as I blew the first note, an old Hasid rose and began signaling frantically to others that they should throw me out of the room. He would have come after me if other Hasidim had not pulled him back to his seat. He had a worried look on his face when he saw that everybody else was also beginning to whistle. It was evident that he had not come to visit for such a long time that he did not know what was now happening at Lubavitch. All through the remainder of the evening he looked around to ascertain whether he had come to the right place. On that night, before the whistling began, we had reached an unprecedented level of intensity. The room was packed to the rafters, and we were singing an up-tempo tune when the Rebbe turned in my direction and asked that I say "*L'Chaim.*" The deputy in charge of wine filled my cup while the Rebbe acknowledged other people's toasts. Then the blue of his eyes came back at me, widening, until I was swept under. I sank below the surface, far beneath the singing throng whose voices I heard only faintly. I drank my wine, and came back to myself, to find his bright face still there in front of me. He brought two fingers to his mouth. I responded with a long piercing note. Thousands joined in, and then the Rebbe, clapping his hands, quickened the pace of the song until it exploded into the noise of war. My guts were hurting from the effort. I had to hold my stomach with my free hand to ease the pain, and to help propel my breath. We whistled down all truthless rumors, as an antidote to falsehood, measure for measure. When we had been going at that maddening pace for what seemed a good fifteen minutes, I had no breath left to give. I was ready to collapse. Abruptly, the Rebbe rested his hands and we stopped. The unexpected ending and the sudden stillness caught us all prancing and snorting like horses after battle. The fluorescent lamps flickering overhead simulated the pallid luminescence of dawn. We stood in the hills of Judea, bathed in the early morning light, gathered around our army chief, from whose holy mouth flew white birds of peace.

Behind that external display of might and the expansive call of our clapping, singing, and whistling, was a pure and concerted desire to cling to God. Our wills exhausted themselves like small wavelets riding up and disappearing into the big breaker. We spent our bubbles and expired within His unity. My legs had lost all materiality, and I had to lean against the wall behind me so as not to lose equilibrium. I felt a dull pain throughout my chest which I then assumed must have been caused by the ribs settling back into place. Giving all of my breath presented me with a new type of consciousness. I might as well have been a new creation. Everyone present looked like pure essence to me.

On the way back home, I realized how we had actually discovered an antidote against vanity, a peculiar one at that, but an effective one nonetheless. We had unveiled the most truthful expression of the self by chasing out the evil wind, the very one that had facilitated vanity's entry, with the wind of our breath. We had, through our selflessness, again made Creation a worthwhile project. If vanity stands for conflict and destruction, we had, through our selfless actions, stood for renewal. For isn't it the *ayin*, the nothingness which is constantly achieved and lived by the *Tzaddik*, the point from which existence took form? As it is said: God created the world out of "nothing." Accordingly, should not the ultimate goal of all humanity be to shed its thickness for the sake of making God known in His own world?

I was musing on those thoughts when I arrived home at three in the morning. Going to bed with so much activity in my head was out of the question. I could not possibly fall asleep. And even if I could, I was not going to put a stop to my joy so prematurely. I sat in silence to delight in the rarest of moments. The morning light caught me wide awake. While I gathered the evidence for an imminent redemption, birds in a tree nearby augured the moment with perfectly rhythmic chants.

Michel ma vie, Meir my light,

With thanks and praise to our Father in Heaven, who answered the prayer of a seventeen-year-old girl: that she may meet the love of her life. You turned up living with your family two doors away from ours.

You were my big brother, my friend, the teacher who connected me to my roots; then you were my husband, and the father of our wonderful children, B"H.

"The Possible Man" was your life's journey, our road map, as we traveled hand in hand; an itinerary for all who would attune our souls to yours.

May your memory bring rich and everlasting blessings to your children, grandchildren, and (already) great-grandchildren.

Your eternally grateful and ever-blessed wife,

Claude Esther Abehsera

76739592R00128

Made in the USA
Columbia, SC
26 September 2019